THE LIFE OF
RYLAN

THE LIFE OF RYLAN

RYLAN CLARK-NEAL

CENTURY

1 3 5 7 9 10 8 6 4 2

Century
20 Vauxhall Bridge Road
London SW1V 2SA

Century is part of the Penguin Random House group of companies
whose addresses can be found at global.penguinrandomhouse.com

Penguin
Random House
UK

First published in 2016 by Century

www.penguin.co.uk

A CIP catalogue record for this book is available from the British Library

HB ISBN 9781780895741
TPB ISBN 9781780896250

Typeset in 12.75/19.45 pt Minion by
Jouve (UK), Milton Keynes
Printed and bound in Great Britain by Clays Ltd, St Ives plc

Penguin Random House is committed to a sustainable future for our
business, our readers and our planet. This book is made from Forest
Stewardship Council®-certified paper

MIX
Paper from
responsible sources
FSC® C018179

This book is dedicated to my mum, Linda Clark.
She's my biggest fucking headache,
but I don't know what I'd do without her.

Contents

'Had a bit of a girlfriend,
bought her a necklace
from Argos'

Ross Richard Clark 1999

1

I was born on Tuesday 25 October 1988 in the Royal London Hospital to my mum, Linda Clark. A good woman – friendly, caring, mouth like a gutter, every other word is 'fuck', but everyone loves her. My dad wasn't at the birth (we'll get back to him later) as he was crashed out drunk on the sofa at home, so my godfather Chrissy stepped in. This may have been a shock to some, but not to my mother.

I lived my early years on Stepney Green Road in East London with my mum, my Nanny Rose and my brother Jamie. My nan was like a second mum to me – and has always lived with us as my mum suffers from severe Crohn's disease. She's always been there for my mum. Especially in later years when we didn't know how this would all turn around . . . she's one of a kind. She grew up during the war, singing in all the pubs, probably showing a bit of ankle, the cheeky mare. I could recite every word to 'Roll Out the Barrel', and to this day I still love a good ol' Cockney knees-up. She taught me well. My brother Jamie is fourteen years older than me. He's been like a second dad to me, or – as you will learn – more like a first dad. He's your typical bloke. Carpenter, plasters walls and ceilings, owns a drill, that type.

We weren't rolling in money as you've probably gathered by this point, seeing as Mum couldn't work due to her illness, but that's where my brother stepped up. He always made sure I had what I wanted, as did my mum and my nan with any money they had. We didn't have loads, but I never went without. I was so lucky to have them. We lived in a terraced council house where you knew all your neighbours. The kind of road where you could leave the front door open, knowing that if anyone dared come in it would be someone you knew. I was the bastard child, that little ginger kid that always wanted to know everything, talk to everyone and get involved in everyone's business. I still am, to be fair . . .

Growing up we were a very close family. One of my

fondest memories took place early one Friday evening. Each week, my mum, Nan, Auntie Sue and a couple of the golden girls (as they called themselves) would go down the bingo on a Friday night. Before each outing they would all come to our house for a Friday night buffet. You know, jacket potato, Batchelors Pasta 'n' Sauce, boiled bacon and salad (because we were well healthy). It was your average Stepney Friday night. I was sat at the table, greedily eyeing up the food, when I heard my mum and Auntie Sue start to argue. Within seconds I could see the both of them pulling each other's hair and trying to rip each other's faces off. I was only young, around seven or so, and immediately started to cry. Our neighbour from next door was round our house and she took me outside to the adjoining park to play catch. I couldn't stop crying as in my head I thought that my mum and my aunt were about to kill each other and I'd be left orphaned. The genuine fear of any seven-year-old.

About twenty minutes later I returned to my house to find that everything was absolutely fine and everyone was sat around the table tucking into their jacket potatoes and Pasta 'n' Sauce. I didn't really understand why it was so calm. But that is just us. Have your row, have your fight, and get the fuck over it. They went to bingo that night and my mum won on the party bingo slots. Only forty quid, but think of the treats we could have for the next buffet. FYI, they fell out over a Quality Street. I can neither confirm nor deny whether the noisette triangle was to blame, but all was now well. Serious stuff.

I went to St Mary's and St Michael's Primary School on Commercial Road in East London. I was a popular kid – surprising as I was the ginger, pasty one, but nevertheless I had lots of friends. I was friends with mostly girls – a few boys, but mostly girls. During playtime, the boys would be playing football, whilst the girls and me would be putting on shows next to the church. Our little dance shows would nine times out of ten revolve around the Spice Girls, and the fight for who would be Geri would arise without fail every break-time. I normally won the fight – playing the ginger card, I got my way. It was around the age of nine or ten that I realised I was different to the other boys. I did the standard . . . Had a bit of a girlfriend, bought her a necklace from Argos, gave her a couple of Happy Meal toys I had doubles of, the usual, but deep down I knew I was a bit different. It wasn't until one evening at one of my mates' birthday parties I really felt it. He was a bit of a cool kid, one of the boys. It was his birthday party and he had it at his house. He had friends from outside of school as he only joined ours in Year Four. Everyone was out playing football, and getting off their faces on Smarties and Asda cola. I was with them, kicking the ball around and getting on well with these boys I'd never met before. After about an hour of playing, I saw my girl mates dancing out in the road. I knew I really wanted to go and join them but it felt nice being one of the boys. As time went on I could feel myself itching to go and dance with them and after about a half-hour I did. Next thing I remember is country dancing to B*Witched's 'Jessie Hold On'. Proper going for it, full out under the streetlights of the council estate.

One of the boys came over and said, 'What are you doing?'

I looked at him (still full-on country dancing) and said, 'It's B*Witched's new song!' He looked at me like I was a donkey with three heads and a handbag, laughed and walked off. I knew he thought there was something wrong with me. But I didn't care, I genuinely didn't care. I carried on dancing with the girls until we all had to go

home and to this day I still smash that routine . . .
Yee-haaaaaaa!

I was a clever child at school, always top of the class
with maths, English, etc., so when it came to applying for
secondary school I wanted to go where all my friends
would be going, which was St Michael's in Bermondsey,
South London, but another option soon came up.

The Coopers' Company and Coborn School in Essex
was a school for really brainy kids, the sort of kids – from
my point of view – you would want to slap. My teacher
suggested to my mum that we should apply for the school
to further my education and swore we would be in with
a good chance. Each year the school would choose
around six or seven kids from the East London area
because the school used to be in Bow. I really didn't want
to go there. I would know no one. The only upside would
be that I would have to get the train to school, and as a
child I was a bit obsessed with the Underground, but is a
childhood obsession enough to start all over again with
no friends? A representative from Coopers' had to visit
my primary school to watch me in class and interview
me. Mr Barry Wellington, a man who looked like he'd
stepped straight out of *Doctor Who*, walked into my Year

Six classroom and started to assess me. It was quite nerve-wracking, and the talk of the class, as my other friends' potential schools didn't do this. I was then taken out of class and into my formal interview with Mr Wellington.

'How are you today, Ross?' he said.

'I'm good, thanks,' I replied. The rest of the interview went well and he left after shaking my hand and telling me that he was very impressed. The next time I saw Mr Wellington was a few weeks later when I was invited for a second interview, but this time it was held at Coopers'. I walked along a beautiful long drive filled with trees and flower arrangements, passing the acres of fields and sports pitches into a paved area called Coopers Court. HELLO! I was more used to an ordinary-looking inner-city primary school – this was something else, it was like inheriting Downton Abbey. I was taken into a grand, lavish reception known as the Foyer, with bottle-green leather chesterfields and a lacquered wood floor that would rival those in Buckingham Palace. In the follow-up interview I was presented with a test. This was the dreaded test I had been told about by my primary school teacher. You fail this test, you don't get into Coopers'.

I found it fairly easy, to be honest, and left feeling excited. Rather than worrying about the test, all I could think of was how beautiful the school was and how lucky I would be to go there. After patiently waiting for several weeks, a letter arrived at my home. The letter was addressed to a Master R. Clark. I could see the excitement on my mum's face. She had failed to tell me what she already knew: if the letter is addressed to the child, it means the child has been accepted into the school, whereas if the child's application was unsuccessful, it would be addressed to the parent. As I opened the letter and saw the acceptance I remember feeling amazing, like I'd done something really good, but at the same time the joy was tinged with upset as I realised I would be leaving my primary-school friends behind.

I don't remember my last day of primary school. Not one thing. Which, as an adult now, I find quite strange, as it's a big thing in someone's life. All I do recall is feeling much more grown-up, knowing I had to get a train to Essex to go to school.

The summer holidays came and went and soon it was nearly induction day. At Coopers' they take uniform to the next level. I was given a full school uniform, special rucksack, which was bigger than me, a cricket kit, a PE kit, a swimming bag and kit, including stitched initials on every garment, not forgetting a tennis racket. I needed a whole new wardrobe to fit it all in.

As I pulled up to the school on my first day, another boy was walking in, also a new Year Seven. We made friends and walked together into the main theatre, which was essentially a grand hall, for our induction with all the other new students. We sat down next to each other and listened to a glamorous head girl give a speech and we learned the school's motto, 'Love as Brethren' and an ACTUAL SCHOOL SONG about the founders . . . I couldn't believe I was going to such a posh school that even had its own anthem! Then the headmistress arrived. Dr Davina Lloyd. A *Dr*! My headmistress was a *doctor*! You could tell she was important by the way she walked and the way she spoke. During her speech she kept mentioning mums and dads. I couldn't help thinking, I haven't got a dad. I hadn't actually seen my dad from about the age of six or seven. I don't really remember him. He was never fully with my mum and things never worked out. He used to visit once or twice a year when I was really young, but then all of sudden it just stopped. I still don't know why. All I remember is he wore this hat and checked blazer and he always turned up carrying a newspaper. I didn't care for Dr Lloyd's speech or my dad at this point though; all I was worrying about was making friends.

I was pleased to see that in my form was another guy who seemed quite chatty with the girls and a bit more on my level, if you know what I mean. His name was James. He was short and fat and I was ginger and pale. The perfect friendship, in my eyes, as if I was going to get bullied at school, I reckoned he would as well, lightening the load. Over the first year we became best friends and spent all of our together. Move over Pepsi and Shirlie, there's two new sassy kids on the block and we ain't taking no shit, sistah!

During Year Eight, my family decided to move from East London to Essex, to a place called Stanford-le-Hope. Before we went, I was still commuting from London to Essex with Ashleigh, another girl from my old primary school. She now went to the all-girls' school close to my house, and one day we decided to jump off the train in Bow on the way home, to walk around the outskirts of the *Big Brother* house. It was just up the road from both our houses and I was TOTALLY OBSESSED with the show. It was 2001, *Big Brother 2*. My fave, Brian Dowling, was in the house. Back then security on the show wasn't what it is now, and you could literally walk around the perimeter of the compound. We decided to pop into the Tesco's that was right next to 3 Mills Studios, where *Big Brother* was filmed, and buy some clothes pegs . . . Why? you ask. We wrote 'Brian to win' on them and wanted to throw them over the *Big Brother* garden wall.

We walked slyly around the compound, thinking we were total James Bonds, looking around to check there were no security guards. The time had come to throw the pegs. 3, 2, 1, THROW . . . ! If that peg managed to get three feet from where I was standing I would have felt like Fatima Whitbread – but sadly it was the shittest throw of all time. In my defence the pegs were really light in weight. Fuck it, we thought, so I just screamed at the top of my voice: 'BRIIIIIAAAAAN!' and legged it. As we were running away, we saw Dermot O'Leary filming *Big Brother's Little Brother* and he shouted to us, 'You're on the telly now!' Dermot was speaking directly to us, and it was the most exciting feeling, but we carried on running. Little did I know that eleven years later he would be standing by my side on one of the most amazing journeys of my life and, not only that, that I would be doing his exact job twelve years later. Crazy . . .

Anyway, where was I? Yes, we were moving from London to Essex. It was hard leaving my childhood home, but it worked better with my travel to school and in the long run worked out to be one of the best decisions we made. My brother's partner Jayne gave birth to my nephew Harvey not long before, making my brother a dad and me an uncle.

At first I found it really hard to deal with. Don't get me wrong, I was completely over the moon to be an uncle and Harvey was absolutely beautiful, but Jamie had always been my father figure and I couldn't help but wonder if that was about to change. I tried not to make it a massive deal and show my family how I was feeling, but it did bubble away in my head for a few weeks, until I realised that the only thing that *had* changed was that we had a beautiful new baby in our family and I knew in later life I could repay my brother by being someone Harvey could look up to. A few years later my niece Olivia came along, making the four of them a proper family.

Back at school I was still relatively new and as a result was bullied a little, especially in those first few years. Me and James would get called 'gay' and 'poof', which looking back on it now, we took quite casually. We would just shrug it off as I guess deep down we both knew we were but didn't really want to fight with anyone because of it. We had a close group of friends including a girl called Katy Thomas, who was quite a shy girl in the beginning, even though she had double-Ds at the age of thirteen – go on, girl! Her mum didn't really like her hanging about with us, as me and James were known as troublemakers. We never meant harm to anyone, but we did like to play pranks and have the last laugh on people.

I wasn't the only one who was obsessed with *Big Brother*. We all were. So much so that during a Year Nine trip to the Isle of Wight (standard school-trip destination) I printed the *Big Brother* eye out from the computer and stuck it on my suitcase. I even laminated it . . . Classy. On my way into school that day a man on the train saw my case and asked if I was going into *Big Brother*. Clearly he was as deluded as I was because he believed me when I said the following, 'Yes, I am. They're doing a special teenage version and I'm going in.' Lying ginger bastard, wasn't I? He congratulated me and got off the train. AND HOLD UP, MYSTIC MEG! Lo and behold, three months later, Channel Four announced a special *Teen Big Brother* series. I should have claimed copyright. To be fair, the bloke on the train might well have been one of my bosses now. Thieving arsehole.

Anyway, as the years went on at Coopers', I started to realise I didn't really enjoy being academic. I loved drama and dance, but the likes of maths and English started to take a back seat in my priorities. By Year Nine, aged fourteen, I knew I was gay. I didn't like girls in a sexual way. Rather than look at girls and think, I want to be with you, I would look at the girls and think, I want to *be* you. It just happened that my best friend, James, was also gay, so it was a lot easier for me to handle, as a problem shared is a problem halved. James's dad, Tony, was brilliant. He was the most understanding father anyone could have and was always on hand to give me advice and help me through whatever problems I had.

That summer, in between Years Nine and Ten, me, James and Katy started going out. We used to get the train into London and go down Soho. For the first few times we would just hang about outside bars and clubs, walking up and down Old Compton Street thinking we were all hard. In reality we looked like silly little kids carrying bottles of Pink Ice and WKD with smug looks on our faces because we'd managed to get served in the local off-licence. One such night, down London, Katy and me decided to try and get into G-A-Y bar. Now G-A-Y was a notorious bar and club on Old Compton Street that looked like the place to be: it always had a queue of cool-looking people that would stretch all the way into Charing Cross Road. There was no way we could get in but I had a little plan. We put on our best blazers and planned a routine we would do whilst walking up to the bouncers. I would make out I was talking into my phone, and Katy would smoke a cigarette. Somehow we thought this would make us appear older, like we were just finishing work and looking to wind down for the evening. By some fluke of life, it actually worked and we were in. We couldn't believe our luck. The adrenalin pulsed through our bodies and the excitement was just too much to handle. We walked into what looked like heaven on earth. A dark club with pink lights, full of good-looking people, and Girls Aloud pumping through the speakers as the accompanying video played on every

TV screen. It was amazing. We drank and danced until the lights came on at 3 a.m. and still, hours later, we were still psyched about getting into the first place, first try and all. We jumped on the night bus home and stayed at James's, as we knew his dad wouldn't have a go at us like our own parents would.

Soon this became a regular outing for us, same routine, same set-up. As the weeks went on, we realised that the bouncers didn't start work until around 7 p.m., which meant if we were in the bar before, we were in for the whole night! Slowly but surely the bouncers started to recognise us as regulars, which meant from then on we could stroll up at whatever time and be let straight in. Weekends sorted.

Through Years Ten and Eleven I was having a great time at school. James and me didn't really care too much. He wanted to be a dancer and I wanted to be a pop star. What could Pythagoras's theorem and Shakespeare teach me about that? We were excluded a few times – once for bullying, which was disgraceful as it wasn't true, but the girl got away with it. She was jealous of our friendship group. I won't go into details as I don't even want to type her name. A few times were for answering back. Every

17

other week, in fact, and all because by this point I had started to highlight my hair. Genuinely. It seemed that girls were encouraged to look like supermodels and boys were encouraged to look like . . . Harry Potter. I never understood the rule. But then there was this other time for having – wait for it . . . my first fight. A real fight. Go on, Rocky! A boy in my class said something to me; I can't even remember now, something along the lines of 'gay boy', and made a limp hand gesture towards me. Normally I would link away and just let it be, because it happened all too often, but something this time felt different. I felt the anger bubble away in the bottom of my stomach – as if my body finally grew a set of bollocks – and work its way up and through my veins, down my arm, making its way closer and closer to my clenched fist, and without even stopping to think I punched him straight in the face. We brawled for a bit but after a few seconds we heard the teacher scream, 'GET OUT FOR YOUR OWN SAFETY' to the rest of our class members. You would have thought there was a bomb. So the whole class left and the teacher locked us in. Great skills, babe. Literally the whole class had emptied and was crammed into the skinny maths block corridor peering through the 20-cm-by-20-cm square safety glass that was embedded in the door. We both looked at each other and, instead of fighting, we started laughing at what had just happened.

That day I was suspended from school and my mum had to come and pick me up; she was so proud that I had finally hit back that she took me to the sandwich shop in Hornchurch to celebrate. As we were walking along the high street, chicken-mayo baguette in hand, a random man walked towards us and said, 'All right, Lin?' I couldn't fully see him at first, but standing there in front of us, I realised, was my dad. He had on the same hat he always wore and the same checked blazer. He gave me a hug and I remember him repeating over and over again, 'Oh, look at my boy, look at my boy.' We spoke for about a minute and then he went. That was the last time I ever saw him to this day. It was strange knowing that was my dad, but you don't miss something you never really had, do you?

Back at school, some of the teachers were so regimented they would have been too harsh for the army. One of the form tutors, Mr B. I'll call him, was so far jumped up his own arse his face was coming back out of his mouth. He would shout, make girls cry, and once even hit my hand away from my face whilst I was scratching my nose. I highly suspected that he didn't like the fact that James and me were gay. In my view he was ultimately another jumped-up homophobic prick. One time he got to me so much that my brother had to come to the school to have a row. We're not a fighting family by any means (except with each other), but if you take the piss, be careful. People like him should *never* be in that job.

One teacher I could rely on was Mr Wellington. Old Barry. He was a genuinely good man and I could always go to him if I had a problem. He would always tell me that what I wanted to achieve in life I would. He not only got me into the school, he carried me through it as well. If more teachers were like him, kids would leave school a lot better off. He shares the same birthday as my mum so I often think about him. I learned that he has recently retired. Definitely a loss for Coopers'. During my final year, James and myself were called into our head-of-year's office. Mr Bamber. By now I was used to him telling us off, so was ready for it. As soon as we walked in, the atmosphere in there felt different, I didn't feel like we were about to get a bollocking. It was the most relaxed I had ever felt in his office. He started by saying that we'd had some great years at the school and had made some amazing friends and memories, but that the school would like to part ways on amicable terms with the both of us and not invite us back to sixth form. James and me started laughing with a sigh of relief as neither of us had intended on coming back. Mr Bamber laughed and made a joke of it as well, and in that moment all hatred that I held for being spoken to like a three-year-old and being told how to look and dress dissolved. James and me knew that for our final term at Coopers' we could be who we wanted to be and do what we wanted to do.

The final few weeks went just the way we wanted. We had fun, and also took our GCSEs. I passed fourteen of my fifteen GCSEs, failing English literature, as I didn't realise when the exam was and decided to go shopping over Lakeside. My last memory of Coopers' was walking out of the school gates with a big old boom-box on my shoulders blaring out Gwen Stefani's 'Hollaback Girl' at full volume and waving goodbye to my childhood. I've got really fond memories of school. I can say that if I were to see 99 per cent of students I studied with out and about, we would say hi to each other. I was incredibly lucky to go to Coopers'. My classmates ultimately were very accepting of me, I made friends for life, and we really all did learn to love as brethren.

'Ryan, Ryder, Rhidian,
Rylan . . . Rylan?'

Ross Richard Clark 2006

2

2005, *16 and Pregnant* . . . Sorry, not pregnant, independent. I'm officially part of the big bad world and doing a bit of modelling in my spare time, nothing special. So what, I hear you ask, is the first thing I do after leaving school? That's right, I go and get a job in River Island. LIVING ON THE EDGE, EH? No, but seriously, I did. The only downside was that the only 'full-time' shift available was 7 a.m. to 11 a.m. working in the stockroom, a two-hour lunch break, then back at 1 p.m. to 5 p.m. on menswear. I didn't care though, I wanted to work. I was quite excited about the idea of working on a till. On my first day working in the Lakeside Shopping Centre River Island store, I made a mate. Sam, nice bloke, worked on menswear, which was where

I was assigned (only half the day, mind), quite stylish, and – by the amount of mascara and bronzer he was wearing and the folded-arm attitude towards 99 per cent of the customers – he definitely liked the boys. First friend sorted. The bonus with having Sam as a friend was that he only lived a few minutes from my house and would drive me home at the end of our shifts. He was the sort of mate you knew you would have around for ever.

One day I had a call from the modelling agency I was working for, doing a shoot here and there. They said they wanted to change my name, as Ross wasn't memorable enough. They chose Keelan. A couple of days later I had a modelling job in London. It was for a concierge company and I had to be the person in the picture delivering some flowers. MADE IT! It was quite a shit job actually, though it paid about £100, which wasn't too bad. But there was a problem. They paid me by cheque, which was made out to a Mr K. Clark. Holding the cheque in my hand I walked over to the woman who had been calling me Keelan to try and explain the mistake. I couldn't possibly cash a cheque to a Mr K. Clark, it wouldn't clear. As I looked her in the face to tell her my real name, I instantly became embarrassed. I couldn't do it. I couldn't face telling the woman

I'd been working with for the past ten hours that I had a fake name. I left the job knowing I wouldn't get paid.

Back at River Island on my lunch break, I popped over to WHSmith's and looked at the baby-name books. I figured to avoid going through 'Chequegate' again, I needed to find a name beginning with R. Ryan, Ryder, Rhydian, Rylan . . . RYLAN? I thought, That sounds a bit like Keelan. And that was it. Nothing glamorous, no elaborate story. That is where Rylan came from. As simple as that, it was settled.

I went back to work and carried on working at River Island, but a few months in I fell quite ill for no apparent reason. I was on the brink of collapse, tired, nauseous, and my vision kept getting impaired. There was no other place for me to go so Linda and me went straight to hospital. We waited until we were seen by the doctor who – *very* casually, may I just add – looked at me and my mum and said, 'We think you may have meningitis.' You what? Menin-fucking-gitis? Are you taking the piss? I couldn't believe what was coming out of his mouth. I looked at my mum who was clearly worried about what he'd just said. He then said that I needed a lumbar puncture. What's a lumbar puncture? I hear you ask. A lumbar puncture is a procedure where a fuck-off needle is injected into your spine to take synovial fluid from in between your vertebrae. 'OK,' I said. I just needed to know whether I was basically going to die or not. It's the first thing I thought. The following day, in walks Dr Whateverthe-fuckhisnamewas. 'Morning, Mr Clark. This is Julia,' whilst pointing to some bird who looked younger than I was. 'All right, Ju,' I said, worrying slightly about the role she would be taking in the coming events. The doctor informed me that Julia herself would be carrying out my lumbar puncture procedure. 'OK,' I said. How could she? *The bird looked twelve years old!* Is this bloke for real? But who was I to argue with Dr Whateverthefuckhisname-was? I was instructed to sit on the bed with my legs flat out in front of me. I was then asked to lean forward as much as I could, which was so painful. It was like Bikram yoga for pain-fetish lovers. Just as I was getting uncom-fortable on the table over walked Julia with a needle longer than my Spice Girl CD collection. She put the needle in my back right at the bottom. The pain was so awful I thought the bastard needle had paralysed me. Actually, scrap that, I sort of wish I did have a bit of temporary paralysis because what she said next nearly did me in. 'Nope, there's none there.' No what, babe? Meningitis? Infection? DVD box set of *Sex and the City*? WHAT, BABE?

'There's no synovial fluid there, Doctor.'

'Try again, Julia,' he said in his monotone voice. She tried again. I was in agony, and lo and behold this time, *nothing again*. Now, wait for it . . . REPEAT SEVEN FUCKING TIMES. That child stabbed her way through my spine seven times to get a drip's worth of this magical fluid. 'All done,' she said gleefully. And done is exactly what I was.

My back was black with bruises and I could hardly move. I didn't sleep that night waiting for the results, I was so nervous, and I'm sure the night porter kept staring at me through the curtain, but I can neither confirm nor deny that rumour. Day three of hospital traumatisation. Results day. In walked Dr Whateverthefuckhisnamewas with little Julia shuffling in behind him. 'We're just going to take a quick blood test,' she said with her sadistic smirk on her face. I swear she was like a devil child. In went another needle into my arm and off they trotted without a single word. Day four now! Day *four*! Four days of this experience and surely now I was finally going to get some answers. In they walked in again, the both of them and now I'm not even naming. He said, 'Well, the good news is you don't have meningitis.' Praise him. He then said, 'But looking at your blood test, you are running low on Vitamin D. Do you get much sunlight?' Much sunlight? It's late November and we're in Basildon, mate, not the Bahamas. What the fuck do you think?

'Not really,' I quietly replied. All I could see was Julia nodding with her smug look.

It turned out I was going to work at 7 a.m. and it was dark, I was leaving at 5 p.m. and it was dark. During my lunch I'd be in artificial light in the shopping centre and I wasn't getting any natural light for, like, ever. So it was all down to that. I asked them what did the synovial fluid come up with then? Now what you are about to read are this bloke's *exact* words, and I quote: 'Oh, we didn't end up getting a lot from that in the end. It was extremely beneficial to us though, as Julia is one of our newest trainees and after doing your procedure she feels a lot more comfortable with her exams coming up over the next few weeks.' I paused. Old Linda paused. After what seemed to me like eighty-seven minutes I said, 'Her *what*?' He looked at me as his proud smirk slowly slipped away. I WAS FUMING! This child had literally stabbed me in the back seven times to get a smiley-face sticker on her coursework. I felt violated. I can't really remember what happened next and I'm not going to sit here and make it up. I'd like to say I slapped Dr Whateverthefuck-hisnamewas and that Julia failed every exam, but I do remember going home and sitting in the garden under an overcast sky in the hope of feeling better. The trauma still haunts me to this day, and whenever I watch Julia Roberts in a film, I think of the child. Chilling.

One afternoon, soon after the ordeal, I was visiting one of my friends at her house. It was a normal day just like any other. I called my mum to come and pick me up late afternoon, which she did. Everything was normal. She arrived and I got into the car and headed home. Everything was normal . . . Actually, no it wasn't. The second I got in the car I just got this feeling in my stomach. It wasn't pain, or indigestion, but this sort of nervous pain. Instantly I knew what was coming. OUT OF NOWHERE I realised I was about to tell my mum that I was gay. Where the fuck it came from I do not know, but I knew it was coming. The journey home to my house was around twenty-five minutes. The whole time I didn't speak a word. I was sweating and felt sick. Why now? Why is this happening now? Just forget about it, I thought. But I couldn't.

We arrived home and I didn't get out the car. I couldn't move, I was stuck, my legs wouldn't operate. 'What you fucking doing?' my mum asked, ever so classily. I didn't respond. 'Oh, fuck ya then,' she said as she slammed the car door and walked straight into the house carrying bags of shopping. Immediately I got my phone out and called a friend and told her what I was about to do. She couldn't believe it – I know, babe, me neither – but she just said, 'Go for it.' I couldn't bring myself to do it though, so I asked her to ask her mum if she could call my mum and tell her. Much simpler. She told me that her mum would call my mum straight away. I was so worried, I stayed on the phone listening to the background noise of her mum making the call. I could also hear our house phone ringing from where I was sitting in the car. Connection made. After what seemed like an hour's wait with my friend on the other line constantly reassuring me that everything was going OK, I heard something chilling. In the background, I could hear my friend's mum let out an almighty 'NOOOOOOOOOOOOOOO, LINDA!'

31

I shat myself. I dropped the phone, scrambled out of the car and made a run for it. I ran for around twenty minutes until I ended up in a field in the middle of nowhere. I had left my phone in the car and didn't know what to do. I sat there for hours worrying that my mum didn't love me anymore. I was thinking about where I would have to go and live, how would I afford it, everything. Everything you could imagine was running through my head. It started to rain, and after another half-hour I finally decided to brave it and go home. I walked up to my house in what seemed like slow motion. I looked in the car to find my phone. It wasn't in there – my mum had obviously taken it in. I knocked on the door and she answered. From the door, I could see that my phone was sat on the window sill. I grabbed it, bolted past my mum and up the stairs to my bedroom, slamming the door behind me. I had a million missed calls from my friend. I called her back instantly. She picked up after one ring and was immediately asking things like where I was and was I OK. I told her I was at home and she seemed relieved. I asked her the inevitable question about my mum hating me and wanting me to get out of her life. She paused.

'*What?*' she said.

'My mum. She hates me, don't she?' I replied.

'Have you spoke to your mum yet?' she said.

'No, why? I heard your mum shout "NO, LINDA" on the phone and figured that she probably hated me,' I replied.

'You fucking idiot! My mum told your mum that you wanted to tell her something and your mum asked, "Has he got a girl pregnant?" She's absolutely fine, you idiot. Let's be honest, it wasn't a massive shock to her!' she said.

I couldn't believe it. I thought she was kicking off about the fact that I was gay, when in fact she thought I'd got a girl pregnant – for fuck's sake, she couldn't have been more wrong. I went downstairs to see my mum. She asked me if I was OK and whether I wanted to talk about it. I simply looked at her like a stroppy teenager and said, 'NO!' and that was it. That's my coming-out story. Every gay guy or girl has theirs and that was mine. I was lucky that mine, although eventful, was pain-free and I'll never forget my mum being the best about it.

A few days after these dramas, I remember returning to work feeling refreshed. Luckily someone had left, which meant bye-bye stockroom and early starts and hello normal 9 to 5. Go on, Dolly. I stayed at River Island for about a year and then moved on to one of my favourite jobs. I started working for Benefit Cosmetics in Debenhams. It felt like I'd been upgraded from cattle to first class. I loved the job, got on with everyone – there were a few arsehole managers in the store, but there always are.

Working for Benefit was amazing – it felt better than being *on* benefits, that's for sure. I could play with make-up all day; that's where I learned how to wear it! I'd have music blaring from the counter (cue arsehole store managers) and just generally have a laugh. Me and Sam were still seeing each other on our lunch breaks which was much needed, and I'd made a few new friends as well, one being Tracey – she worked on the nail bar round the corner from my bit. A really sweet girl who lived round the corner from me as well. That was me lift home sorted, when Sam wasn't about. We got to know each other pretty well and we would all go up the pub in my local town and have it up on karaoke night. I'd always sing Santana's 'Smooth' whilst she always sang 'Black Velvet'. We had some great times. That is until about six months in at work when I got the sack. It wasn't my fault. But actually, it was.

In Debenhams they have 'Mega Days' – a special discount day for store-card holders. Someone I knew came in. Rather than give them 30 per cent off, I gave them 50 per cent. I remember the cosmetics manager called me into the office. She sat me down and asked if I'd been giving out discounts that I shouldn't have. Obviously I lied and said I hadn't. I was feeling confident I'd got away with it, but then she pulled out my till records. It was like an episode of *Judge Judy*. She said I had two options. 1: I could leave. 2: I could go for a disciplinary hearing and get formally warned. Great, I thought. I'll take the warning. I love my job. But then she said, 'And because you're seventeen your mum will have to be present for it.' Fuck that, Linda would kill me. So I left the job I loved there and then. Brucie Bonus was I still had about twelve demo products in my apron so I left there about £350 up. So, you know, swings and roundabouts.

So there I am. Jobless. Seventeen and jobless. Thinking about it now, that's not that unheard of, but I felt dirty for not being in work. One night, up the pub, the manager, Lee, offered me a job. Me in a pub pulling pints? Really? The only thing I'd pulled up to this point was a few muscles in the stockroom and some rejects on nights out. I took it. I was one of Stanford-le-Hope's finest pint-pullers – or so I'd like to think, but it's my book so

I'll say it. Working at the Inn on the Green was brilliant, and as you've come to learn by now I was always more interested in making friends, and the pub was no different. I started going out with Lee and Sam from River Island. We were the three gays. We used to go to this place called Colors in Basildon. It was about fifteen minutes from our houses. It was a gay club above Basildon market. The glamour. For all its faults (and believe me, there were so many), it was a right old laugh. It's the sort of place where if you ended up being sick on yourself lying on the dance floor, the fellow revellers in their Kappa tracksuits and knock-off UGG boots from the market wouldn't judge you, as we didn't judge them. The music was brilliant. Dirty, cheesy pop. People would get up on stage doing the dances to Girls Aloud (badly) and we would dominate the two poles on each side of the dance floor. I miss that place. It really was the best night out. Pretty soon James and Katy from school started coming out with us. Together we had a going out schedule. We would all go to Romford on a Tuesday night for 'gay night'. Friday we were back in Colors for 'gay night' and Sundays we'd go to Chicago's in Chelmsford for 'gay night'. We were gay night veterans. Weren't we worldly!

I would LOVE nothing more than to tell you some of the funnier stories from our nights out but I couldn't do it to myself or to any of them lot. I do remember (vaguely) that after one particular night out we got in a cab home. I'd been drinking rosé wine and sambucas all night, the perfect mix. Whilst travelling along the A13 I was sick out the window. Seeing as we were doing 70 mph it didn't really matter as it just flew away. It wasn't until we pulled up outside my house and I opened the door that I found the mix of sambuca and rosé was splattered all along the cab, and because we'd been going at 70 mph it had somehow managed to *strip the paint* off the car! I want to say I paid the cabbie, but I more than likely did a runner.

But the night I do vaguely remember was the night I met my first boyfriend. He was tall (which for me was touch, seeing as I was six feet three) – we clocked each other over everyone else's heads on the dance floor. Let's call him Mr S. He was a really nice bloke. Older than me – I'd just turned eighteen and he was twenty-seven, I think. It might seem strange, but in my defence I've always looked and acted older. He treated me really well. He even had his own place in Southend. A real catch. It was important to me that my friends liked him, and they did, especially as we always thought James's house was haunted and Mr S did a bit of ghost-hunting. This was enough for us all to decide to do a seance round James's. It freaked the life out of us. James's kitchen drawers would open and close by themselves, and believe me it wasn't his Dalmatian dog Domino. If it was, we would have put him on *Britain's Got Talent*. Doors would slam and floors would creak on their own, but when you openly asked for it round that house, you *always* got what you bargained for.

There was one thing I absolutely couldn't do with my new boyfriend and that was introduce him to my family. This would have been the first time I've ever 'brought someone home' and I just couldn't do it. My mum was great, and so was my family, but the problem didn't lie with them, it was within me. I didn't feel comfortable doing it. I think because I had worked myself up so much over the years to the point of actually telling my family that I was gay, it had been such a build-up of emotions, that now there wasn't anything to hide in that way. Deep down maybe I liked keeping a part of my life still secret. We stayed together for about six months and split up because I wasn't ready for a longer relationship. If he reads this, he will know who he is. I do know that he has since moved from Essex and has a child with his new partner. I wish them all the love and luck in the world.

'The password is
"watermelon".'

Big Brother 2007

3

So now it's 2007, I'm eighteen years old, single, and working in a pub, and three guesses what I'm *finally* old enough to do . . . That's right: apply for *Big Brother*. My ultimate dream. And that's exactly what I did. I remember walking into the ExCeL Centre in London's Docklands and coming face to face with thousands of other hopefuls all wanting to get into Britain's most famous house. I looked like a child compared to some of the other wannabes surrounding me. I was given a sticker and to this day can still remember the number: LB247. Being a geek I worked that out as London, Day 2, Number 47. That's a Coopers' Coborn education right there.

I was stood in a group of ten people. The bloke

auditioning us had a stamp with a *Big Brother* eye on it. He said that this was our chance to impress him and to move through to the following round. He asked us questions in the group to see who would disagree or agree with whoever's answers. I remember piping up about something or other and the next thing I knew I'd got the *Big Brother* eye stamped on my hand. I felt like I'd won the lottery. The next stage was to go upstairs and fill out the application form. Now this was no ordinary form. This was the *mother* of all application forms. It was fifty pages, front and back. It took over two hours. Things like: 'Can you draw where you see yourself in six months?' Obviously I drew a picture of me winning *Big Brother*. (Coopers' education kicking in again: art award.) Once completed, I handed it in, and they said they would be in touch.

A month later the phone rang from a private number. I answered it. 'Hello, Rylan, this is *Big Brother*. You are required to meet us on Tuesday morning at 9.30 a.m. at Oxford Street station. Look for a man with a green umbrella. The password is "watermelon".' Then they hung up. Was this a wind-up? Is it someone taking the piss? Tuesday came and I got on the train and headed to Oxford Street station. Nine fifteen a.m., there I am, dolled up to the eyeballs, looking for some big old green umbrella. I felt like it was an MI5 mission. Nine thirty-five a.m., I still can't find him. Clearly shitting myself thinking: Is this a task? Have I missed my chance? That's when a guy walks up to me and casually says, 'Hello, Rylan. What's the password?' Me being all savvy, and thinking it's the press, ignores him because he's clearly not carrying some big old umbrella. He asks me again and I tell him, 'Fuck off, I don't know what you're going on about.' I was getting irritated. As he walks off looking confused, I see a little green umbrella dangling from his wrist, the sort you'd find in the pound shop, which wouldn't even cover your eye if it was pissing down. I ran over to him, screaming at the top of my voice, 'WATERMELON! WATERMELON!' and explained the confusion. We shared a little laugh and he led me into the Cumberland Hotel. We walked down the stairs to the meeting rooms. The thought had passed my mind that he could be a murderer or a ginger-hater, but I'd coloured my hair dark by this point and he wasn't going to do much damage with the pound-shop umbrella he was carrying, so risk duly assessed, I went for it.

I was taken into a room with nine other applicants. I was

given my sticker to put back on, LB247, and joined them. Their stickers were all different. There was LA, LB, MA, MB, NA, NB, EA, EB, etc. Two people from different UK cities from different days to ensure we hadn't met at auditions – very clever, Big Bro. There was a long table of about seven people. They introduced themselves as the producers and pulled out a box. A real standard DIY box, nothing as glamorous as one would expect from a show that looks so slick on TV. It was a bit of a let-down if I'm honest – where's the glitter, *Big Bro*? One explained, 'In this box there are ten different scenarios that all start with the words "Most likely". What we want you to do is to come up one by one and pick a scenario out of the box randomly. 'We then want you to line the rest of the applicants up in order of "most likely" to "least likely".'

People started to do the task – things like 'Most likely to start an argument', etc. And how it worked in practice was that a person would go up and pick from the box, read the scenario, order the rest of us in a line, place themselves in the line, and only then would the other applicants find out what the scenario was. I was last. I walked up to the box and pulled out the scenario. I got 'Most likely to become a housemate.' It was easily the hardest one, as this was the one scenario they'd all travelled here to actually be in, and I was putting the hopefuls in order. I lined them all up and put myself right at the end. Most likely. After my task scenario was read to the group, the girl at the other end looked at me like I'd robbed her newborn. The producer gave me a cheeky wink though.

I left there feeling good – you could have pissed on me even though I wasn't on fire and I *still* wouldn't have given a fuck. Shit on me, however, then we've got a problem, which one particular pigeon felt he had to do with me – right outside Oxford Street station. OK, so I was annoyed, but in all fairness, bird shit is supposed to be lucky, and I needed a bit of luck – though what I didn't need was *actual shit* on my crisp black blazer. I was so embarrassed – people were looking at me and thinking, You have shit on your blazer. Then something completely unconscious happened. Whilst knowing *exactly what I was doing* physically, my brain couldn't stop me from doing what I *knew* I was about to do. I looked at the shit on my lapel and slowly felt my hand lift towards it. My fingers extended, poised and ready, and I wiped it with my finger, then raised my hand to my mouth and – in the heat of the moment – licked it. *Why* I did it I don't know, but I was

46

now not only embarrassed but I also had the taste of pigeon shit in my mouth – which, for reference, tastes like a Duracell AA battery with a hint of foot . . . The fact that bird shit on me was deemed lucky made the whole situation slightly more acceptable.

Anyway, a couple of months had passed and I'd heard nothing. Surely they wouldn't leave it this long. Until one day the phone rings. Private number. I started shaking. I knew it was the call. I made sure I looked half decent in the mirror in front of me (God knows why, it's not like they could fucking see me down the phone) and I answered, 'Rylan speaking,' in my deep telephone voice.

'ROSS! You've left them fucking straighteners on again! *What 'ave I told ya?'* It was my mum from the house phone. We're ex-directory. Another month had passed and another withheld number rings. Thinking it was my mum, as by now it almost always was, I answered.

'Hello, Rylan. This is Big Brother. You need to be at Victoria station, platform six, at nine thirty a.m. on Tuesday. Look for a man with a green umbrella. The password is "Evian".' The phone then disconnected. I couldn't believe it.

Tuesday came round so quickly. I got on the train and

got to Victoria station, time checked 9.25 a.m. I looked around for a bloke with a green umbrella. I spotted him straight away. I slowly walked up to him, checking to make sure no one else was watching, and I looked him directly in the eyes, standing there all suited and booted. Slowly and knowingly I said to him, 'Evian.' He looked me up and down and, in the most Cockney of accents, replied, 'Who the fuck do you fink I am? W. H. fucking Smith?' Now this bloke is either really unhappy in his job or I've totally got the wrong person. Just as this thought raced through my mind, a man walks up to me and says, 'Hi, Rylan.' It's the same bloke from my Oxford Street rendezvous, with the same umbrella! I felt like such a prick.

He walked me to a nearby hotel and explained that I'm about to see the show's psychologist. The last thing I wanted to do was fail this bit! I was taken up in a lift to the ninth floor and walked to room 908. He points at the open door, and all I can see is that there's a guy already sat down. His name was Gareth. Scottish. A rather lovely bloke, actually. As we sat down he asked if I wanted a cigarette and from that moment I knew we'd get on well. Deep down I knew this had to be the last stage as I'd calculated that the series was due to start in about four weeks' time. After about an hour of talking, it was time for me to go and I stood up to leave the room. He looked up at me and said, 'Fuck me, you're tall. You're going to find it really small when you go in there.' Right then, I froze. Did he just say what I think he just said? WHEN? WHEN I GO IN THERE??? He backtracked and thanked me for coming. As I was taken down in the lift I knew I'd got it. I just knew. Two weeks later I was working behind the bar and the phone rang. Withheld number. I ran outside to the beer garden, midway through pouring a pint. 'Hello, Rylan, it's Suzy from *Big Brother.*' Wait!! This woman is talking to me like an actual person – have I done something wrong? 'Rylan, we would love you to be a housemate in this year's *Big Brother.* Congratulations.' I literally fell backwards. 'We will be picking you up from your home address tomorrow morning at ten a.m. and taking you into hiding before the series starts. You will need to pack everything you wish to take into the *Big Brother* house, including any toiletries. If you forget anything you will have to order products on the house shopping list and we cannot guarantee certain products will be in stock.'

What was I hearing? I was an actual, real housemate.

That little ginger kid on a school trip to the Isle of Wight – with the homemade *Big Brother* eye sticker on his suitcase, lying to people on the train – could foresee the future. After I hung up, I went back into the pub and told Lee. Everything had to happen quickly, and I explained that I had to leave there and go home and pack. It was a Friday, the busy shift, but he let me go.

I got home and realised I had no clothes. I didn't have any money either. My Auntie Sue lent me £100 and straight away I called Katy and James so we could go to Lakeside. We had a right old spending spree in Primark: pants, socks, T-shirts, *the lot.* Seeing as it was my last night of freedom, there was only one place I wanted to go with James, Katy, Lee and Sam. COLORS, obviously! I got so drunk. I kept thinking, I'm gonna be famous so this is the last time I can go out and get fucked without people taking photos of me. Sad bastard. That was probably the funnest night out we'd ever had and James and Katy stayed at mine which made me feel so happy and sad at the same time. They left at 9 a.m. the following morning. At 10 a.m. on the dot my chaperone turned up. Rob, his name was, very quiet. We packed the case in the car and my mum asked him where I was going. He

THE LIFE OF RYLAN

wouldn't tell either of us. He took my phone off me, I said goodbye to my mum and got in the car.

I followed the signs all through the journey and around seven hours later we arrived in the Lake District. A small hotel called Cragwood Manor in Windermere. I checked in, had a vodka Appletiser and went to bed. When I woke up the next morning, Rob took me through what was going to happen. 'Each day I will give you something to do: think of it as a little mini-task. It's for your "house-mate pack". We'll also be filming your profile VT.' Excitement.

A week and a half had passed and I was still there. I knew the series was starting, but I was still holed up in the Lake District. Launch night was fast approaching and I was still there. On Wednesday the official launch night, I asked Rob over and over again what was happening but Rob wouldn't say anything. At 9 p.m. I'd had enough. I told Rob I was going downstairs for a cigarette. Surprisingly he let me go. What he didn't know was that I had already sussed out that in this hotel if a room wasn't occupied, the staff left the door ajar. I crept into an empty room and turned on the TV. I watched a house-mate enter the house I was supposed to be going into.

Her name was Laura; she was Welsh and seemed bubbly. I panicked and quickly left the room to go back to my room as I didn't want Rob to clock what I was doing. During the next ninety minutes I went for about eight cigarettes. Each time creeping into a room to watch around four minutes of *Big Brother*. But then I noticed something. Each time I saw someone going in it was a woman. No men? It started to make sense. No men were going in tonight. It made me feel a bit more relaxed about being at this hotel in the middle of the Lake District.

'When are we going back to London, Rob?' I asked, fed up, but again he stayed silent on this matter. So, me being Miss Marple, I faked another cigarette break, but this time I crept down to the hotel reception. There was a smart-looking girl working the evening shift, so I gave her some elaborate story about how Rob was my boy-friend and how he had planned a surprise holiday for me, which was so nice but that I wasn't sure when we were leaving, which was so inconvenient because I was actually trying to arrange a birthday surprise for him when we got back. Without flinching (I wasn't sure she was even listening) she informed me that we were check-ing out the following morning. Pushing my luck even further, I told her that I was trying to arrange this surprise party for him but didn't want to use our room phone as he'd obviously become suspicious, so if I could use the phone in her office to make a call, I'd be ever so grateful. She happily obliged and I called my mum. Firstly she had a go at me for ringing her, but more importantly she told me that the first man would be entering the house on Friday night. *This made sense!* Analysing all the information I now had, I knew that we would be checking out tomorrow morning, travelling back to London to possibly stay in a hotel nearer the house, and I'd perhaps be in the house by Friday. BRUCIE! The next morning, to my complete non-surprise, Rob woke me up at 7.30 a.m. and told me we were leaving. 'Oh, really?'

We travelled back and I was now taken to a hotel near Watford and a short while later two women came in the room dragging a big box. I knew what was coming – my willy went a bit funny. IT WAS THE FUCKING *BIG BROTHER* SUITCASE I'd always longed for. There it was in all its glory: black, glossy, and a hard case – HARK AT ME with a hard-case suitcase. Makes a change from the 1970s floral fabric ones my mum had knocking about in the loft. I remember saying to them, 'Even if I don't go in, I've got the suitcase!' to which they giggled. I was taken to a room which had a fake diary room set up. I sat down. And then the voice of Big Brother said, 'Hello, Rylan. You now have thirty seconds to explain to your potential fellow housemates why they should pick YOU to join them in the *Big Brother* house. Your time starts now.' I shat myself. the thought that at this stage I might not even be a housemate made me feel sick. But then I remembered, they don't know that I know they're all female. I've got an advantage here. So I said, 'To all the girls, I'm a make-up artist, I've got shit-loads of make-up and beauty products, etc.' The klaxon sounded: time up. I was escorted back to my room feeling sick.

I woke up the following morning still unaware of what was going on. A producer walked into my room and sat me down. She said there had been a change of plan and that unfortunately I wasn't needed at the moment, but not to rule out going in later on in the series. I was devastated. I couldn't believe what I was hearing. She finished by saying I could keep the suitcase. All that was going round in my head is what I said the day before. I felt like a mug. I got in the car with Rob and he handed me my phone back. I had a nervous feeling it was all over when they let me have 'contact with the outside world'. I went home so deflated. The following Tuesday, 5 June, my phone was ringing off the hook. It was 6 a.m. It was practically everyone I knew calling me to say that I was in the paper. I ran over to the shop opposite my house and there I was. Front page of the *Daily Star*, main head-line: '*Big Brother*'s Secret Weapon Revealed.' I stood there in shock. That's when I knew I definitely wouldn't be going in, as back then, if you were found out, you defin-itely didn't go in, later on in the series or ever!

I laugh about it now, as 5 June is also my brother's birthday. He was on site doing some building work when he was greeted with all his macho mates holding a copy of the *Daily Star* which read 'Bitchy gay wannabe Rylan Clark is set to spice up the *Big Brother* house' Very proud moment for my macho brother. What better way to get a birthday present from your little brother so publicly? Happy birthday, Jamie.

'Then break a fucking leg . . .'

Rylan Ross Clark 2008

4

A year had passed. I'd been given a job by one of my friends working for a shop in Lakeside. It didn't end too well there though – as after about four months of working on the shop floor, a glass pane fell out of a window and cut the top of my left arm open. My initial thought was the sadness that one of my favourite shirts was now ripped, but it wasn't until I saw the blood that I realised it was more serious than a slashed T-shirt. I ended up with a thick three-inch laceration across the top of my left arm, a speedy trip to the hospital and returned to work the following week. To cut a long story short ('Where there's blame there's a claim'), I left and settled out of court with the company and lived the following couple of months without too many money worries and a bit of a sore arm.

This bought me some time to try and get into something I really wanted to do, but it was hard and something was still playing on my mind. Every single day I woke up, genuinely hurting that it never worked out with *Big Brother*. It didn't feel right. I *know* I was supposed to be in that house. So many questions were running through my mind. Why was it taken away from me? Whose fault was it? I tormented myself so much that I felt like I was going insane. Luckily my friends were always on hand to make me feel better. One Tuesday night we all decided to go out. Two guesses where . . . ROMFORD, OBVIOUSLY! GAY NIGHT, BABES! It was standard classic night out with me, James, Katy, Sam, Lee . . . the crew. And that's where I first met Mr H. I saw him standing at the bar. He was looking at me and I was sure he was giving me the eye. That or he needed a patch, I wasn't sure.

As all this was going through my head, he came over and we started chatting. We clicked almost instantly and quickly became a couple – there was no asking if he'd go out with me, or wondering if he fancied me, we just went for it. We started dating and it was all going well. It was a Thursday night, he turned to me and said, 'Do you want to come back to my house and meet my parents?' THE 'P' WORD! Oh God, I thought, what do I do? We got on the bus and made the very short journey to his house, two stops I think. All that was running through my head was fear. Would they like me? Will they think I'm an idiot? We turned up at his house; I remember walking up to the door and slowly walking through. His mum and dad seemed really nice. Fear unloaded.

That night we ended up staying awake until 2 a.m. talking, all four of us. During our seven-hour chat his mum was talking about how she also grew up in the East End of London, and we started to talk about people we might know in common. It's well known that people who lived in East London during certain eras would have known or known of each other's families. You know, the famous old East End line, 'Oh, yeah, darlin', I knew the Krays' – that sorta thing. She was talking about a guy she used to go to school with. She then said one of the strangest things, anyone has ever said to me. She told me his name. I froze. That name rang every bell with me. It was my dad. After asking more questions and finally understanding the full story, it turned out she went to school with my dad. I was gobsmacked. The man I don't really know anything about, the potential mother-in-law apparently knew better than me. It was weird but as always I dealt with it.

A few days after the in-law meeting, I received a phone call from an agent asking me to go in for an audition for a boy band. I rocked up to the meeting and was told that the job was located in Ibiza for a year's contract the following year. I instantly turned it down. As much as I would have loved to have done it, I'd just started a new relationship, and I was obviously very serious about it because I remember I was more than happy to give up on a job to stay with him. Little did I know when I met him, but THIS BOY would be the one I'd introduce to my family. My first one. I wanted my mum to meet him. I took Mr H to a family party, which was a big deal for me. And it turned out it *so* needn't have been. It felt totally normal and even old Linda liked him. Win-win. Come November, Mr H announced out of the blue that he had signed up to do panto in Durham, where he was cast in the main role – playing Aladdin. I was disappointed as it meant he would be away for a few weeks running up to

Christmas, but by this point I felt secure enough in our relationship to let it go. We had a little send-off party around James's house – nothing too extravagant, his family, my family and a few of our friends. It was a nice affair and I felt genuinely gutted that I wouldn't see him every day for a while. Two weeks later and myself, his mum, his dad and granddad had a great idea. We decided to drive up and see him in the panto. I was excited, but less excited at the prospect of my six-feet-four-inch body crammed into the back of a Ford Ka whilst sitting on his granddad's lap for six hours. But I did it. In the name of love.

I remember it clearly. We were about an hour away from the house he was sharing with the other dancers from the panto; the iPhone had just come out and I was playing with the Maps app, thinking I was all hard. I was so excited to see the dot move and be so close to seeing him. After six hours in the car (and possibly giving my future granddad-in-law a lap dance or two), we arrived. It was mid-December and I remember all the houses had Christmas lights and decorations sparkling outside them. As we walked up to the door it opened and out walked two guys smiling at me, heading off on their way. Obviously people he is sharing the house with, I thought. Then I saw him. I was so happy I could have cried.

He introduces me to two of the girls he's also sharing the house with – both of whom seem lovely. I sit down as he's going to make us all a cup of tea, when I see on the side of the chair an iPhone. 'Is this your one?' I shout to him in the kitchen. 'Yeah, ain't it good!' he replies. Whilst I was holding it to look at the cover, it lit up. A message from someone popped up on the home screen saying . . . 'Was that him? I feel a bit bad now?' (Sent 2 minutes ago.) I froze. What the fuck is that all about? Along the bottom of the screen the silver bar was shimmering with the words 'Slide to read.' Glowing like a neon light. So what do you do in this situation? Suddenly I feel like there's something dodgy going on. Is this about me? So I did what any self-respecting human would do . . . I SLID TO READ! And there it was. The whole conversation between my boyfriend and the boy I've just said hello to walking out of the front door as I was walking in. Messages along the lines of 'I really enjoyed holding you in my arms last night,' and my favourite, 'He won't find out, he's up the other end of the country lool.' The prick couldn't even spell 'lol'. So there I am, hours away from home, his mum opposite me, his dad next to me, and his granddad sat in a rocking chair oblivious to everything (you couldn't make it up).

I walked up to Mr H in the kitchen and asked him to come upstairs because I needed to talk to him. We walked up to his bedroom, the place in which I'm sure he's been cheating on me. I held up his phone, clearly showing the messages, and asked, 'What's this?' He looked at me for what seemed liked five minutes, grabbed the phone and uttered the words that I knew would cause the first relationship heartbreak of my life: *'Well, I've not been happy for a while now . . .'*

I went into shut-down mode. He didn't even try and lie his way out of it. And on top of everything somehow it was all my fault. I remember slowly walking down the stairs, step by stomping step and up to his dad. I asked him calmly if he would drop me at the nearest train station. Weirdly he didn't question me or hesitate as he made his way to the car. I kissed his mum on the cheek, thanking her for being so welcoming of me. I shook his granddad's hand and walked out the front door. 'Wait!' I heard Mr H shout from the doorway. I turned around walked up to him, toe to toe, and asked him, 'Do you have a performance tonight?' He looked at me confused and answered, 'Yes, why?' I looked him up and down, knowing it would be the last time I'd ever grace his presence and replied, 'Then break a fucking leg.'

I walked the short distance to the car feeling like Peggy Mitchell, sass central. And away we drove. The drive was only ten minutes and it wasn't until I was nearly at the train station that it started to hit me what had happened. I said goodbye to his dad and watched him drive away. That's when I got really upset. I walked to the ticket window and asked the ticket man for a ticket to London. 'Where?' he said, completely uninterested. 'Anywhere in London, please,' I replied, physically shaking. 'That's £105 then.' I put in my card and it declined. I only had £100 on my card. I pleaded with the bloke, I was clearly in a state, but he didn't give one fuck. A woman wrapped her arm around me and said, 'Here you go pet,' and passed me a fiver. I don't know who she was but I wish I did because she really helped me out when I needed it. Thank you, whoever you are.

I boarded the train to London and spent the hours travelling weeping silently in my seat. It was a lonely

Christmas that year. Nothing had changed, I still had all my family and friends around me, but I didn't have Mr H. I found it really hard. I just couldn't wait until the holidays were over. March came and I stumbled upon the boy on Facebook Mr H had been cheating on me with. I was sure of it. I did what any other scorned woman in her right mind would do – FACEBOOK-STALK THE BAS-TARD. After doing a bit of digging I found a picture of him with the panto cast, my ex-boyfriend included. At first glance I didn't see it properly, but after a few seconds and a forward lean into the computer screen I saw it. He was playing Jafar in the panto. JAFAR! MY BOYFRIEND CHEATED ON ME WITH JAFAR! *Do me a favour!* They were an item now. Good fucking luck to them.

A few days after my Facebook-stalk session I received a random phone call. 'Hi, Rylan. My name is Mark and last October I was putting together a boy band you were sup-posed to audition for. The one based in Ibiza. Anyway, unfortunately one of the boys has dropped out and I was wondering if there was any chance you would like to join them. Rehearsals start next week in Manchester and then you would all fly out three weeks from now. Are you up for it?' The first thing I thought was no – but then, hold on, I wasn't working, I love singing and dancing, and I'm bored. I had no intention of spending the year in Ibiza. I thought I'd go to rehearsals, fly out there, have a nice, free two-week holiday singing and dancing, get homesick and fly back. After all, it's not like I'm in a relationship or anything, is it? 'I'd love to, mate,' I replied. I found out two of the boys, Danny and Lucas, were northern, and me and the other guy were both from Essex. Brucie Bonus. The local boy was called Terry and I got in touch so we could drive up to Manchester together for rehearsals. He was an unreal singer and we had good banter. Danny was a proper Manchester lad, loved a bit of Oasis and played the guitar. Lucas was a Yorkshire boy; he was gay and liked Girls Aloud. So not only did I feel like one of the lads, but also had a gay BFF to do routines with!

We started rehearsals for the show not too long after we arrived. We were to perform two shows on the island. A Westlife and a Take That tribute show. I was bang up for it at this point. Learning all the routines thinking I was Robbie Williams in 'Could it Be Magic'. It was great. At the end of our first rehearsal we put on a sort of mini-show in a social club just outside of Manchester. The average age was around seventy-six, so we weren't hoping for a standing ovation or anything like that. Nat King Cole probably would have gone down a bit better, but we did it anyway. We were so shit, if I'm honest. Fucked up every move and couldn't stop laughing the whole way through. We still had a lot of work to do but we were determined to get there by the time we hit the sunny shores.

On the final night before me and Terry headed back to Essex, we all went and stayed at Danny's house. It was one of those proper bonding moments. Danny played his guitar while we all sat around the kitchen table, smoking and drinking, singing along and making up songs as we went along. I started to really like these boys; it had only been a week but weirdly we started feeling like a proper unit. I quickly realised that I couldn't just go out there for two weeks and let them down, as I'd planned. It would really spoil things for everyone, including me. If I was going to do this, I had to do it with all my heart and soul or it wouldn't be worth it. This was a serious opportunity. So many questions ran through my head. Am I really going to be living on the island of Ibiza? I don't even really want to go, do I? But looking around the kitchen that night, seeing all three of them so content, I had to do it – not just for them, but for myself. I needed to grow up. I was twenty years old and had never left home. I'd had a few jobs but nothing too serious. If I was to grow up, this would be the last time I could do something like this. And secondly, if I was to really grow up, this opportunity could be the making of Rylan. Was it time to let Ross take a back seat and let Rylan take the lead? I think so . . . And so 4bidden (with a 4, because we were well cool) was born.

'4bidden . . . with a 4'

Rylan Ross Clark 2009

5

Vengaboys' 'We're Going to Ibiza!' on repeat, literally the whole run-up to leaving. I'm going to Ibiza, party capital, island of dreams, and I'm getting paid for it. Woo-hoo! Touch.

The day had come to pack up my troubles in my trusted ol' kit bag and fly away. I arrived at Stansted airport and met up with Terry. Luke was flying over from up north and Danny was driving out as we needed a tour car. But before our Ibiza party could start, we had to fly to Mallorca as we still had another three days' worth of rehearsals. We were back together as a group and practising our routines – just a few more days and we were good to go. Because Danny was driving the car, we had to get the ferry from Mallorca to Ibiza, and management thought it would be funny to book the 6.05 a.m. ferry after a full night out boozing in Magaluf. All I remember is boarding the boat and collapsing. Two hours later and we were there. It was fucking muggy out, I'll tell ya. Still in last night's jeans and sweating like a glass-blower's arsehole, but we made it.

We started the twenty-five-minute drive to San Antonio Bay. Seeing as we didn't know the island, we ended up going the non-scenic route through the hills. The whole time I was trying to spot where the beach was, and whether our new apartment was close to it. We finally arrived outside El Jardines del Albaicín. It was an apartment block of six apartments – no pool and the '*jardines*' were literally a tree and some shingle outside each downstairs apartment. It was your classic Balearic white-rendered shell, with bits of render missing from the façade, and to really set the ultimate holiday experience scene, a lone washing machine sat proudly outside under the sun with nothing but a foreign brand of detergent named Colon perched proudly on top. I didn't like it, there wasn't a pool, and it looked a bit shit in all fairness. The homesickness began to creep in. Already!

The block was actually owned by our management

and – may God strike me down – this was the list of residents. In our apartment was obviously us (Take That and Westlife). Above us was Kool & the Gang, in the two apartments next to us were Robbie Williams and the Drifters, and the two others above us were Abba and the Chinese acrobats. I shit you not. GENUINELY this was now my life. Waking up in the morning for a cheeky cigarette, seeing a Chinese bloke above us balancing on the edge of his balcony on a broom handle by his chin. For real. The apartment was dated and in serious need of a revamp, but who am I to moan? We didn't have to pay for it.

We settled in and it wasn't all that bad, Luke and me shared one room while Terry and Danny shared the other one. The gays and the straights. We're so multicultural. After an hour's sleep to catch up we decided to go for a little walk around to get our bearings. We were on the bay side of San Antonio, a ten-minute walk to the big clubs and the West End. A one-minute walk around the corner from ours was a long strip of bars and the beach. Thank fuck. Myself and Terry had a little walk along and a blonde woman pulled up on a moped outside the bar closest to us. It was called Bucanero, and it looked like a pirate ship on crack. Gotta love a theme bar. She pulled off her helmet and said, 'All right, boys.' Terry went all shy because he blatantly fancied her but I went straight in with, 'All right, babe. You all right?'

She smiled instantly, knowing I wasn't a threat, shall we say. Her name was Candice, she owned Bucs. Really nice girl, bit of a ladette with a broad Grimsby accent. We explained we were living out there and that we were in a boy band. She told us where was good to go and where wasn't. She was a top lass and I knew we'd get along.

We didn't start work until the following week so we had the first week to settle in and rehearse. Bucs became our local and we loved it in there. It genuinely was the best bar on the island. I grew really close to Candice pretty much straight away. As much as I loved the boys, I needed that girl mate in my life and she slotted in perfectly. I remember her saying to me that very first week, 'Listen, babe, when you leave at the end of the season, that is if you last that long, if I don't cry, please don't be offended. I've been doing this for ten years now and I'm used to making friends and seeing them go, so just to let you know.' You could see it was built into her, to have fun, make friends, but ultimately to never get too attached. I just laughed at her, but I could understand that; people come and go all the time, it's not worth the upset.

A few nights before we were due to perform our first show, me and Terry got a bit brave and decided to go to Es Paradis. One of the 'big clubs' on the island. I remember it was a Tuesday and we rocked up to the front of the queue thinking we were famous and walked straight in . . . Only because Candice knew the door staff and texted them for us, but the other clubbers didn't need to know that. We walked straight into the VIP balcony and sat down. We had virtually zero funds. We'd scraped together twenty euros and bought one drink each. Terry started chatting to some girls who left after ten minutes (nice one, Tel), but they left half a bottle of Grey Goose behind. NICE ONE, TEL! We sat down and poured a vodka. I'd noticed this bloke down on the dance floor. Very nice-looking. I kept looking at him. He kept looking at me. Terry turned to me and said, 'He's your type, ain't he?' He was, in fact, my type. Dark hair, tall features, fit body etc., but all I thought was that he was one of the girls' boyfriends and he was going to stab us.

Twenty minutes later we were chatting to some people on the table next to us and I turn round and see this guy

THE LIFE OF RYLAN

ten feet behind me. He had made it up to the VIP area. I froze. Is he gonna stab me? Is he gonna stab Terry? Is he . . . giving me the eye??? No way. He was WAY out of my league. All of a sudden something came over me (no not in that way!), I mean I felt a bit of courage start to come up from my stomach and out of my mouth. I don't know if it was the Goose talking but I turned to him, grabbed the bottle and said, 'Fancy a drink?'

What?! What the fuck are you doing?! Well done, mate, it's all over before it's even begun. You had a life to lead! I thought as the words left my mouth. He smiled coyly. 'I'd love one,' he replied. I've been here four days and I've turned into Casanova.

He joined our group and we started chatting. Turns out he had been out on the island for the past few years running the strip club in the West End, an area around San Antonio, notorious for bars, strip clubs and all-round general weirdness. He was in charge of managing the club and casting all the girls. At this point Terry's ears pricked up, shock. Terry instantly wanted us to get married. In all fairness he was really nice. Funny, charming and up for a laugh. It was about 4 a.m. and as the lights came on we swapped numbers. Genuinely, girls, you know that fear, you instantly hide your face thinking, OH GOD, THE LIGHT, THE LIGHT! AM I PATCHY! DO I LOOK LIKE PEGGY PATCH??!?!?

He turned and said, 'I'd better go grab my flatmate before she walks out and can't find me. I'll meet you out front.' As the club cleared out I waited with Terry outside. I couldn't find him. We waited nearly an hour before I realised I wasn't going to find him. There were just too many people. We slowly walked home and went to bed, worn out. The next morning I woke up, no text, no missed call, nothing – a blank screen. I walked outside, cup of tea in hand, and sat in the garden. Terry had already let the others know that I was upset I didn't get to see this bloke from last night at the end. I couldn't stand it anymore. I decided to text him. A casual text, hope you're OK, etc., nice meeting you, blah blah blah. The message didn't deliver . . . Danny decided to ring the number from his phone on a private number. Then this happened. 'The number you are calling cannot be recognised.' You've got to be winding me up. I've took his number down wrong, can't remember his name, NOTHING.

I'd saved him in my phone as 'Mr Sin', and believe it or not neither me nor Terry were sober enough the night before to remember that he said he worked in a strip club. FUCK YOU, GOOSE! How on earth am I gonna find this bloke on an entire island? However, I am not beaten easily. There were us four boys, the Drifters, Robbie Williams and a Chinese acrobat, all on different laptops trying to find this bloke. With no luck. By 4 p.m. I gave up. I'd called his number twenty times just to hear over and over again that it wasn't a real number. I felt like shit. It's only four days into a nine-month stretch and I've already mugged myself off. Great.

With nothing more to be done on locating Mr Sin, me and the boys focused on rehearsing for our Westlife show. Halfway through 'Bop Bop Baby' my phone rang. The screen lit up with the words 'Mr Sin calling'. I dropped the mic, Luke turned the music off and I froze. 'ANSWER IT!' Danny shouted. I picked up the phone . . . 'Hello?' I coyly said.

'Hi, mate, how are you? Have you been trying to ring me?' he asked.

I coolly brushed it to one side and said, 'Yeah, once or twice,' not wanting him to know I had a team of tribute acts trying to locate his position on the island, and his shoe size . . .

He laughed. 'I've just managed to turn on my Spanish number because I still had my English sim in the phone. It's working now. I've just had a text message saying twenty missed calls from your number.'

I literally died. How the fuck do you recover from the dreaded 'twenty missed calls' text? Fuck you, iPhone. 'Oh, really?' I said. 'Must have been an accident.' The ground could have swallowed me up and sicked me back up again and I still would have felt the shame running through my body.

Obviously he didn't feel the same, as he asked me out on a date the following night. We met at a place called Sunset, a strip of beach outside legendary bars like Café Mambo and Café del Mar. It was amazing, my first official Ibiza sunset. We strolled along the beach, which could have easily been lit by a professional lighting team. The sand looked burnt orange underneath the glow of the Balearic sun slowly setting. We watched it drop beneath the ocean's horizon as the bars behind us played meticulously timed chill-out music to coincide with the disappearing orb in front of us. As a surprise, we strolled back to his apartment where he prepared dinner for me. He was half-Italian and made the best lasagne. He was a true gentleman, Linda would approve.

I plucked up the courage to tell him about the crack team from the previous day and we both laughed about it. I finally worked out why he was saved as Mr Sin. The name of the strip club he ran was called the Sin. It was like cracking the Da Vinci code.

I'd only been on the island five nights, but already I was seeing someone. Over the next few days, me and the boys started performing. We were a bit ropey at first but we soon put on a really good show. We quickly become one of the best acts on the island and we were working nearly every night. I was getting paid to have fun, was finally seeing someone who was good to me, and generally I was having the time of my life. Great.

A month or so into our popstar adventure I noticed that Luke was hitting it hard with the all-night parties, to the point where some nights we would have to cover for him in our show. He was a great singer but it was like he was throwing it all away for a drink. One morning we staged an intervention and sat him down and told him that he needed to sort himself out. Not only were we worried we would get sacked from venues, because by now the show was starting to look a bit shitty, but more importantly we were also worried for him, as he was really going hard at it. I said to him, 'If you can handle going out all the time and still perform the shows, then fine. But the day we have to cancel a show because you can't make it on to the stage and you lose us money, that will be the day that we book your flight back and you're off home'. We wanted him to know we were serious. We didn't want this to fuck up. We worked two or three hours a night and were some of the best-paid workers on the island. We had a great deal. I felt it was worth him knowing that. He promised us he would sort himself out. A few weeks later it happened. Luke turned up after a night out to our apartment at 4 p.m. He was completely out of it – couldn't even speak! We knew there was no way to do the show with only the three of us because of the choreography. We didn't have time to re-choreograph the whole show in a matter of hours. We had no choice but to cancel the gig. For me that was it. We'd warned him. We called the management and explained. They booked his flight home and the following day he left. I looked at him sadly, as I knew that he had fucked up an opportunity that could have been an amazing one for him, not just now but for the future. The thing is, I didn't even want to come here originally, but even through the homesickness I knew that it was where I was supposed to be, and I was gutted for him because, deep down, he knew that was true for him too.

Now we were a man down. For a few days we did the show as a three. We had to. Management were sending a replacement but he wouldn't arrive until the week after. It upset me to think that we'd started this experience together but that we wouldn't all finish it together. I was also worried how the new boy might fit in and whether we'd like him, or if he'd even like us, but luckily Candice was always on hand for a chat. I would see her every day. She had become one of my best mates there and she always spoke the most sense out of everyone.

Then Adam turned up. He was about ten years older than the rest of us but he was a right laugh. To see us in a line-up we were all so mismatched, but that's what was great. We were all so different that it worked well. Adam slotted in like a dream and 4Bidden actually with four members was back on its feet.

One of my favourite places to perform was Charlies Bar in Es Cana. It was a gorgeous beachfront bar and the crowd in there was always amazing. One night whilst doing the Take That show I spied a girl in the audience who I was sure used to go Coopers'. It's that feeling, isn't it? You know when you're abroad and you see someone from home? You feel like you've just invented air! It's SO IMPORTANT to make a big deal and go over and be like, 'OMG, how are you? What are you doing here?!' SO exciting. Her name was Charley and she was in the year above me, but we'd always got on well.

She introduced me to her friends she was out there with. Lucy, a singer, who had also performed out in Ibiza the year before, and Lucy's mum, Tracey. They were a great bunch. Charley was also a singer, so during 'Relight My Fire' we grabbed her up to be Lulu. Believe me, that's an honour. The two weeks that they were out there in Ibiza, I felt like they were my best times.

I was halfway through my Balearic dream journey and I couldn't help feeling slightly homesick. It's not like I wanted to go home but I kept thinking about my mum. It always worried me that something would happen whilst I was away, and with her being sick often I was always on edge. Thankfully she was OK, but I still worried about her. I missed my friends too, Jamie, Katy, Sam, Lee. Deep down I knew I had to see this experience out.

And I wanted to. All I had to do was consider my life for two seconds. Me and Mr Sin were in a fully fledged relationship. We were like the Posh and Becks of the island. He knew everyone out there and ran the strip club, and I knew everyone and was in the boy band. I was earning money, doing something I love, making new friends and had my own Italian. Bargain bucket to the good life!

So much can happen on a small island. For example, there was a lady called Jackie who was brilliantly amazing. She ran one of the venues where we performed. She was in her late forties early fifties – Scouse as you like and mental. I remember her saying to me that this island will get inside of you. You won't want to leave it. And she was right. I didn't want to leave. I had it all, why would I want to leave?

That is until one morning me and the boys woke up to find our front door was wide open. This wasn't too unusual as some nights we would most likely leave it open, pissed, but this time something wasn't right. I looked around the room for my cigarettes, I went to grab my sunglasses to put on to go out (always looking like Jackie Stallone), but I couldn't find them. I thought one of the boys must have had them. I walked into Danny and Terry's room. They were half awake and I asked where my glasses were. Now, my little joke, whenever I can't find anything, is I shout, 'Someone must have stolen them!' Danny screamed, 'Someone's stolen them, Rylan!' and I started laughing. Little did we know that our perfect Ibiza bubble was about to be well and truly burst. My glasses, Terry's laptop, Danny's credit card, gone. We couldn't believe it, let alone understand it. This may seem like common knowledge to anyone to lock your doors, but it wasn't like that where we lived. Everyone knew everyone. We called the police but they didn't understand us and we didn't understand them. In all fairness, they didn't seem to care that much. We found out that Danny's credit card had been used in a shop in the West End, so we ran there. They didn't have security cameras so there was no way of finding out who it was. All of our songs were on Terry's laptop, along with other stuff we needed. During all of this I had a feeling that we wouldn't get our stuff back. It wasn't life-changing but it was a fucking bastard to deal with. We all had our suspicions that it was someone who lived in our compound – and to this day all four of us still think it's the same person – but we could never prove it. A few days later that certain person, along with the rest of their band relocated to Mallorca. Coincidence, eh?

We managed to sort out all our songs and luckily it didn't mess us up our routine too much. We carried on as normal. We were good at our job, super professional, but still managed to have fun along the way even if we'd been thieved of all our worldly possessions. As the season was edging ever closer to the end, it started to dawn on me that it would not go on for ever. Mr Sin and me decided that we just lived too far apart to make things work in the UK, and decided that it was just an island romance. I really have a lot of respect for him. We had our highs, lows, something in between, but overall he was a really nice person. If I was to see him now I'd definitely stop and say hello. There's no bad blood between us. Which for me was unusual. I was used to being fucked over, but he changed that. I really hope he's happy. There's so many stories from that island that I could tell you, but I would have to write another book. I really grew up. I finally became Rylan. That's all people knew me as. So many people would say to me, 'One day you'll be doing this on your own.' Not to discredit the other boys, but I guess, in a nice way, as a credit to me and what I was doing. I also learned how to use a washing machine . . . Only in Spanish, but still, I did it. I made so many friends along the way but the best friend I found was Candice. She looked after me so much, she was like a big old Grimsby sister to me.

On our final day I remember packing my suitcase and saying goodbye to our friends. I said goodbye to Mr Sin, which was bittersweet, as I was upset to say goodbye, but so happy to part on such great terms. I remember giving old Jackie a cuddle and remembering her words from earlier on in the season. Ibiza definitely is a part of me now. And finally I said goodbye to Candice. I walked up to her outside Bucs and she looked at me. As I stood there looking at her she turned away and walked down the side of the bar to her office. I walked in and there she was, crying her eyes out. She was just as shocked as I was. 'In ten years no one has ever done this to me,' she wept. We both stood there crying like a pair of soppy pricks. I couldn't help but smile and have a little laugh, remembering what she'd said so early on in our friendship. I was flattered to be the one she broke for – not in a sadistic way but more in a genuine way. She said that she would miss me, and I said the same right back. I knew we would

Nice hair, Linda.

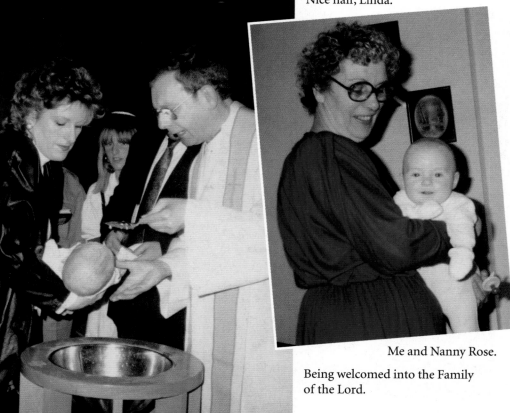

Me and Nanny Rose.

Being welcomed into the Family
of the Lord.

Butter wouldn't melt.

Me and ... Santa?

Look at the mop on that!

West Ham Fun Run '96!
Up the Hammers!

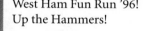

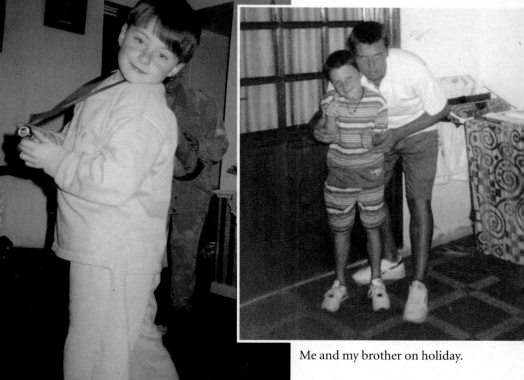

Me and my brother on holiday.

Lime green Bon Bleur tracksuit…
My mum must have known.

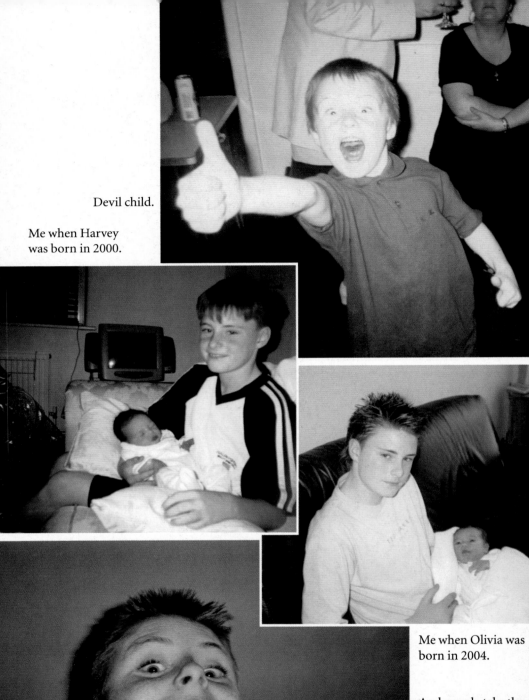

Devil child.

Me when Harvey was born in 2000.

Me when Olivia was born in 2004.

And people take the piss of what I look like now...

Mates holidays, I look like a toilet brush!

Me, James and Katy in Kos, the state of us!

Because we're well hard.

4Bidden with a 4. Because we were well cool.

Boyband days with Candice.

'Flying Without Wings'

Classy outfits, only the
best for 4bidden.

Casual Ibiza nights.

Me and Lee on one of our nights out.

Me and James doing…
fuck knows…

The EsseX Factor judges.

definitely see each other again, but it would never be the same. We cuddled for what seemed like an hour and then I left. As me and the boys jumped into our car for the very last time, it hit me. We all took one last look at our apartment – I wasn't going to miss the Jardines – and set off for the airport. The thirty-minute journey went so quick. I spent the whole time thinking about what I was going to do when I got back. I didn't have a job, and in reality I hadn't saved as much money as I should have done. I was worried, but I wasn't going to let the worry ruin our last ride together. We pulled up to the airport. Danny left the car there as management were going to pick it up at a later date, and we all headed into the terminal. Adam was also from up north, just like Luke, so it was nice that there was still the north/south divide in our group. It was like a final scene from a movie. Danny and Adam's flight left at 12.05 p.m., Terry's and mine left at 12.10 p.m. The departure gates were next to each other. The four of us stood there, under no illusion that we hadn't performed together for the last time. Although there was drunken talk through the season of 'When we get home we can carry on and get a record deal, blah blah blah,' we knew this was it. We hugged. As the northerners walked towards their plane, us southerners walked towards ours. As I walked up the stairs from the tarmac and arrived at the door of the plane, I turned around. I looked at the island for one last time. The end to another chapter of my life. I took a deep breath in, closed my eyes and smiled. The island would always be in me. And 4Bidden (with a 4, because we were well cool) was over.

'The winner of 'The Essex Factor' is . . .'

Rylan Ross Clark 2010

6

October 2009, fast approaching my twenty-first birthday and hot off the tarmac from the time of my life, I decided to arrange a party. I'd saved a couple of grand from the band but I still didn't have a job. I didn't let it worry me too much, but in the back of my mind I knew I had to do something. It was hard going at first. It was quite an adjustment from working every night doing a job I loved on an island where the sun always shines to being back in Blighty.

Seeing my friends, my mum, my nan, my brother and everyone I loved reminded me how much I'd missed it all. It was nice. My nan had moved in with my Auntie Susan. Sue lived in a bungalow, so it was a lot easier for my nan to get around. My nan has always been like my second mum and always lived with us, but I totally understood. I knew it was going to be hard not having her at home with me and my mum, but thankfully my trip to Ibiza and my new-found independence made it easier for me to deal with mentally. I felt a lot more grown up and had experienced not having them around me 24/7. This time I couldn't be selfish; this is what was needed to make my nan's life easier.

I had my twenty-first birthday in a hotel in Essex. It was nothing grand, just a nice family and friends mix. The invites were all boarding passes, a reminder of my time in Ibiza, so that was my little nod to the band. Adam and Terry turned up, but Danny couldn't make it, which was a real shame. It was a great night – everyone had loads to drink and the music was amazing. We did the standard twenty-first birthday décor, with pics of me as a baby sprawled over the walls, and we even brought our promotional boy-band posters back from the island – they made a cheeky appearance next to the stage area. Got to love a bit of self-promotion. It was so lovely to have my family and friends all together in one room after what seemed like a lifetime away.

October passed and it was time for me to get a job again.

I wanted to perform but it's not that easy, is it? I passed my driving test and decided to go back to Benefit Cosmetics, but this time working in Boots in Chelmsford. I fitted in well with the girls in the cosmetics department; they all loved having a boy work on the counters. I was back to doing a job I used to love – just don't bring up the fact that I was sacked the last time from Debenhams; somehow I managed to get away with it. One random Sunday in November, Terry called me and asked if I wanted to go and support him at a local singing competition at Chicago's in Basildon. I wasn't doing anything in particular and thought it would be nice to see him and his family, so I did. I turned up in black skinny-fits, a white T-shirt, a leather jacket and sunglasses . . . It's November, but that's just me. The competition was called 'The Essex Factor' and worked exactly the same as *The X Factor*. There was auditions, if you were successful you would go through to a boot-camp round a few weeks later, and then six weeks' worth of live performance shows at Chicago's in the New Year where the audience would vote each week.

I walked in and went over to him. I sat with Terry's nan, mum and brother whilst waiting for him to audition. I felt a little tap on my shoulder. I turned around, and standing in front of me was a woman with a fur shawl, pink lipstick and white-blonde hair. For a second I had no idea who it was, then she said, 'Rylan, it's me, Tracey – Lucy's mum, Charley's friend – from Ibiza.' It was Tracey! I gave her a cuddle, and we laughed about the times we would get her up to be Lulu during the show in Charlies Bar.

'What are you doing here?' I asked. She informed me that Lucy was a judge so she was here to watch her. It was like a little Ibiza reunion. I gave Lucy a kiss and watched the auditions. She was a really good judge, dishing it out. Go on, girl. One of the judges came over to Tracey. A guy named Lee, he was the organiser.

'Who's this rock star then, Trace?' he asked. I turned around, looking for whoever this bloke was talking about. 'I meant you,' he said with a grin on his face.

I introduced myself and Tracey explained what I did. He said that I should audition and I laughed and said that I was there to support Terry. He left it at that. Tracey kept pushing me to audition but I didn't feel comfortable without the boys; I felt weird at the thought of doing it on my own. Terry got up and smashed it. After a few drinks, Tracey finally persuaded me to audition. I was the last person on. The only backing track I knew was Lady Gaga, 'Bad Romance'. I got up, Dutch-courage style, and went for it. The music began and the Gaga in me came out. I pranced, I strutted and I hip-popped my way through the next two and a half minutes. The crowd were cheering and I was slightly pissed, a lovely combo. They couldn't get enough. I could see Lucy giggling the whole way through. 'You're through to boot camp!' they said in unison. What have I done? I was only here to support Terry, and now I'm through to boot camp. What the fuck does that mean?

Come January, all fifty people who got through the auditions were invited to boot camp. Now, in all honestly, it was in a village hall in the small town of Laindon in Essex. It looked a bit naff but I was there with Terry and we had a laugh. We were put into groups and asked to perform on a stage, the usual. It was to the same format as *The X Factor*, minus the big arena. I got through, as did Terry, and we were assigned Lee as our 'judge'. We were through to 'live shows'. What this meant was that people would buy tickets to come to watch and then they would cast their vote on their favourite.

At the end of the six weeks, the person with the most votes would win £1,000 in cash and gigs all across Essex. It was a brilliant deal. I got really close to Lucy and Tracey, to the point where I was seeing Lucy more and more each week. Lucy and Charley were in a duo themselves, called New Shoes, so I would go and watch them perform with my mates. Each week we would all meet at Chicago's and rehearse on a Sunday afternoon, ready for doors to be opened at 6 p.m. We had a photoshoot, and VTs recorded to play before our performances. It all looked very professional and completely mimicked the real *X Factor* 'package' a contestant would hope to be a part of.

The surprising fact was that hundreds of people came every Sunday to watch the 'live shows'. I somehow managed to sing and dance my way through to the final. All of my family and friends came to watch. The night had a Michael Jackson theme and I was assigned 'Thriller' as my song choice. I had a troupe of twenty dancers and we were all dressed as zombies. The production was on point and the place was completely packed out. The atmosphere in the room was tense and electric. Watching everyone else perform made me really proud – all the other finalists did a great job. It was widely speculated that it would be a two-horse race between myself and a girl called Aiesha. She was UNREAL. I'm gonna sound like Louis Walsh, but she was like a little Whitney. The audience were given voting cards and it was all down to them. After an hour and a half waiting, the votes were finally in and the results were announced. Lo and behold, myself and Aiesha were the final two standing. This was it. 'THE WINNER OF "THE ESSEX FACTOR" IS . . .' I didn't win, I came second. It didn't matter. I'd had such an amazing laugh performing each week, PLUS Aiesha was amazing and really was a well-deserved champ . . . Something which I thought I'd left behind in the Balearics, I seemed to find back home. I wanted more.

After the competition ended, I became good mates with Lee who was always encouraging me from the day I met him at the auditions. He started booking me gigs. One gig was in Scotland. In fact it was a woman who used to come and see me in 4bidden in Ibiza who wanted to book me to perform for her and her friends at a social club. Her name was Margaret and she was a lovely woman who must have watched us in the band about a hundred times over the summer. I was shocked. They paid for our flights, accommodation, and I was going to get paid on top of that. Looking back now it wasn't tons of money, but I didn't care, I was treated like a celebrity in the town of Stirling. About a hundred people turned up to the gig in which I sang about twenty songs over the course of two hours and had my lightbulb moment. This is what I really want to do. I loved my job at Benefit, but I know that performing is everything I've always wanted to do.

So without further ado, I quit my job at Benefit. I went back sometimes, to do little bits and bobs in between whilst I tried to gig. Lucy and Charley always helped me out when they had gigs. I would tag along with them and sing a few songs, just put myself out there and eventually get myself solo gigs. The only problem was it wasn't paying the bills. I was lucky my friend Helen owned a photographic studio: she gave me work airbrushing photos for her, which I was a natural at. She helped me when I needed help and I'll for ever be grateful to her. I worked with her for about a year. Some gigs came up but nothing major.

'I should have been a better friend and I wasn't.'

Rylan Ross Clark 2010

7

Later that year I did something I regret to this day. On a night out with my mate Sam, he told me excitedly that he'd started seeing someone. He seemed loved up and I was made up for him. We were like the Lone Rangers out clubbing it up every Sunday, so when he told me he was seeing someone it was like one of us had won the lottery. A few weeks later, he called me, asking if I wanted to go round his house and meet his new boyfriend. I couldn't wait, you know that feeling when you go and pass judgement and give the whole 'If you fuck my friend over, I'll kill you' speech. The best thing about meeting your friend's other half in my opinion. Anyway, I drove round to his house and went in. His name was Mr A – older than us, nice-looking; I felt like I'd seen him somewhere before. But where? It was just the three of us. We all had a few drinks and I remember we were all sitting in the lounge watching stupid TV. There was something a bit odd about the situation. I didn't know what it was but I just felt that it was a bit wrong. It got to about midnight and randomly Sam decided to go to bed, leaving me and Mr A in the living room. We were all a bit pissed but it did seem weird that he went to bed and Mr A didn't follow.

We carried on watching TV. I was lying on one sofa and he was on the other. After a few more drinks I felt his foot touch mine. I just thought it was an accident. Again a few minutes later he did it again. That definitely wasn't an accident. I looked at him and he sort of smiled at me. My stomach went funny. If he hadn't been one of my best mate's new boyfriend I would have definitely gone there. What the fuck is going on? Why aren't I jumping up and asking him what the fuck is wrong with him? We stayed up until 4 a.m. I don't even remember talking to him. I got off the sofa and thought that I needed to leave rather than stay because I didn't trust what might happen. I'd never do anything to hurt my friends, especially one of my best ones.

I stood up and said I was leaving. He asked why. I felt myself quickly make up an excuse, that I'd just remembered I had to work the following day. He sort of smirked and leant towards me and kissed me on the lips. I just froze. What the fuck is he doing? Why the fuck haven't I punched him directly in the jaw? I did nothing. I just walked out and went home. I felt sick, not because of the drink but because I felt I'd done something wrong. Even though in fact he was the one who'd crossed the line

I didn't know whether to tell Sam. I hardly slept that night. The following morning I had a text from a random number: 'It was good to meet you last night. Hopefully we can see each other soon.' Is this a set-up? Surely this isn't real? It was him. But now I couldn't bring myself to tell Sam. I felt dirty. I wish so, so much that right there and then I'd picked up the phone and called Sam to tell him what was going on. But I didn't.

After a month or so, I'd heard that they'd split up. I never found out why, but that's when the texts started to pour in. Mr A would text and ask to see me. There were loads, messages saying he couldn't stop thinking about me, etc. Again, perfect opportunity for me to tell Sam, or at least fuck Mr A off and be done with it. But I didn't. There was something I liked about it. I found myself texting him back. After a few weeks of texting, I managed to convince myself that now I wasn't doing anything wrong. With hindsight and on paper, I guess I wasn't doing that much wrong. He wasn't with Sam. He was single and so was I. But still, deep down, I knew it was gay code. I shouldn't.

We finally met up. I told no one. He was everything I wanted him to be. Charming, good-looking; had his own place, etc. I really started to like him. All the while I was still convincing myself that I was doing nothing wrong. He would tell me that he was falling for me and could see a future together. I believed every word, totally blinded by his charms. I was leading a double life. A single one when I was around Sam, and the life I really wanted when I was around Mr A.

It was an early Sunday morning when I was lying in bed and heard my mum let someone in. She called me down and told me to get up. I crawled out of bed looking like Cher on crack and shuffled down the stairs. I walked to the garden, grabbed a cigarette and lit it. Sam walked out to me. In that second, when I looked at him, I just knew. He looked me up and down and said, 'I know.'

I just froze, still half asleep, but all of a sudden so awake. 'What you going on about?' I asked.

He only had to look at me to see I was lying. I was shaking, he was shaking. 'Have you been seeing Mr A?' he asked.

I just looked at him. I could have lied. I could have told him that nothing was going on. I could have said whatever I wanted. But I owed him the truth. 'Yeah, I have, and I really like him. I'm sorry.' With that line he walked out of my house and out of my life for ever. I never had the chance to fully explain to him what had actually happened. I broke the code. Completely. I accept that. But that, genuinely to this day, was the last time I ever saw Sam. One of the best friends I ever had.

The only thing keeping me going was Mr A. When Sam came to see me, he was on holiday and was back the following day. I just couldn't wait to go and see him. The following day I texted him as he landed and asked what time I should come round. I'd been to a local card shop that made handmade cards and had one made with 'Welcome home' on it. He texted me back saying he felt really tired and could I see him the following day? Something didn't feel right. I drove round to his house and parked a bit along the road. I texted him asking what he was doing, with his house in clear sight. He told me he was in bed and practically asleep. He wasn't. I could see his lights were on and he was moving about in there. I waited ten minutes or so with the card in my hand, sat in the car. I was going to surprise him but couldn't understand why he was lying. A few minutes later I saw a guy walking up the street in a checked shirt carrying a bottle of red wine. A gay guy I recognised from around. He walked up to Mr A's door and rang the bell. Mr A opened the door and kissed him. Not a 'How are ya?' kiss. A proper kiss. I walked up to his window, prancing on tiptoes, looking like Foxy Bingo. I manoeuvred my way past an electricity box and perched gracefully but sharply behind a bush. I couldn't tell you what type of bush, but it was a bushy bush. I looked up to get a better view and the perfect angle so I could peep through his Venetian blinds and see the two of them kissing inside. My heart just sank. I've lost one of my best friends over you and now you've done this to me.

I felt like I'd lost everything in the space of twenty-four hours. I walked back to the car to go home. I saw the card on the seat. I hadn't written in it at that point. Rage slowly came over me. I grabbed a pen, wrote a message, walked up to his door, placed the card on the doormat, rang the bell, walked back to my car and drove off. The message inside the card read: 'Welcome home, Mr A. Make sure you don't spill red wine down that checked shirt, it's a cunt to get out.' And that was that. Good riddance, Mr. A.

I've never spoken to Sam since, and to this day, on my life, it's one of my biggest regrets. I should have been a better friend and I wasn't. And if you ever read this, I am truly sorry. I wish you so well in life, and thank you for being a great friend. I just wish I was a better one to you, and I miss you.

'OK, I've seen enough.
Time to get your kit off'

Katie Price 2011

8

It wasn't until March 2011 that I decided to try and go back to modelling. I found a casting call for a new modelling TV show. It was quite vague. It just said that the auditions would be at Westfield London and it was an open casting call – no brief, no specific look, nothing. I decided to go. I arrived at the super shopping mall for the first time and saw that in the middle was a stage set-up and a catwalk. There were also TV cameras surrounding the stage and a judging table with three seats. As I turned around, that's when I saw it. A twenty-foot photo of Katie Price with the words 'Signed by Katie Price' printed along the bottom. It's Katie fucking Price's new show. I loved her. I once got her to sign her book for me over Lakeside.

I queued up and got an audition number. There were about a hundred other hopefuls all crammed in a make-shift enclosure. A runner asked me to go upstairs and film a little intro video, which I obliged. As I was making my way up the escalator and making small talk, that's when I saw her. Katie Price was coming down the esca-lator adjacent. She looked straight at me. Genuinely, out of all the people around, she looked straight at me and sort of smiled. Either that or it was a Botox lapse, but I still stand firm that it was a sort of smile. My willy went funny – it's the same type of funny when your belly feels like jelly.

After filming a short video I was asked to go to an audition. I stood behind the automatic doors which led out to the white gloss LED catwalk, waiting in anticipa-tion. All I could think about were the other auditionees. All really pretty girls and guys . . . well, they all looked like Dreamboys. Six-packs, pecs bigger than Katie's newest tit job. I didn't fit in here. What the fuck was I doing?

Before I had time to chicken out, the doors opened. A crowd of about a hundred people started clapping and I strutted for my life. I remember doing the most muggy of muggiest things ever, and when I reached the end of the catwalk I did this sort of pose where I pointed to the camera with my thumbs up with a slight smirk. MUG CENTRAL.

Time for the judges to speak to me. Katie was sat alongside two men. One guy called Bayo, a model-agency director, and Glen, a TV producer.

'What's your name?' asked Glen in his monotone voice.

'Rylan,' I replied, fearing my life was in danger.

'How old are you?' Bayo excitedly asked.

'Twenty-two,' I recited.

And then Katie said the following. 'OK, I've seen enough. Time to get your kit off.'

You what, babe? Time to get my . . . What's that now? Little did I realise that part of the audition was to walk back through the doors, remove your clothes and walk out in your underwear. I felt like I'd just been kicked in the bollocks with a trainer made out of a cactus.

I felt myself smile and walk back through the doors. Why am I doing this? Am I really going to walk out in the middle of Westfield in my underwear? I haven't even tanned my legs. Then the unthinkable happened. I did it. Before I even let the thought process to develop fully, I was standing unclothed, in my underwear, slap-bang in the middle of Westfield. The crowd was cheering. Clearly giving me props for being the skinny, lanky prick among the buffed-up gym freaks.

The judges smiled, I made them laugh a bit and the next moment, 'You're through to boot camp,' the judges exclaimed . . . I've heard that before, I thought. (And, in actual fact, I'd hear it again the following year . . .)

I went home feeling good, although a little bit exposed, shall we say. A month later it was time to go to boot camp. I remember it really clearly, as we had to make our own way to a manor house in a place called Frome. It was Glastonbury weekend and it wasn't far from where we were heading. The trains were filled with one of two types of person, the model type – pouting, putting on lots of make-up and scared shitless about what the weekend would hold, or the Glastonbury type – pissed, ungroomed and pissed a bit more. I fell somewhere in between.

I didn't know what to expect that weekend, but it certainly started with a bang. We were asked to turn up in 'glam evening wear'. Lots of girls in skin-tight bandage dresses, and guys all dapper in their suits. I turned up in black skinnies, boots and a feather shoulder blazer. Standard daytime wear.

About seventy wannabes were parading around outside this beautiful manor house. The cameras were set and it was time to start. Out walk the judges. 'Hello, contestants. After much deliberation we have decided that we have put too many of you through. If we call your name, please make your way into the manor. If we don't, it's back on the coach to the train station, I'm afraid.' Someone please tell me this is a wind-up. I've travelled five hours in a feather blazer through pisshead central to get here. Katie started reading the names. Renay, Hannah, Jay, Jemma, Melissa, Amy, Kirsten . . . Numbers were quickly falling. False nails were being bitten. It was tense. The judges were each taking turns to say a name, very slowly.

Katie grabbed the list, smiled, the same sort of smile I thought she gave me on the escalator . . . or is it the Botox again? 'RAYLEN . . .' she said loudly. People looked around. Is it me? Did she mean me? 'RAILING,' she corrected herself. Again . . . does she mean me? Glen, the other judge, then said, 'Rylan.' Thank fuck for that. I pranced around in my feather blazer with a sigh of relief.

As I walked in, Katie mimed the word 'sorry' to me for getting my name wrong. I didn't give a fuck. I was in.

As me and my feather blazer strutted through the hallway of this grand manor, I knew this was going to be a laugh. I made mates with most of the forty contestants that were remaining. We all had a welcome drink and some time to get to know each other. One of the guys was a really loud Geordie guy called Jay. Tattoos head to toe, eight pack, he was massive. We got on instantly, telling jokes and taking the piss out of each other remorselessly.

The producers came into the room we were all in and told us that the boys and the girls would be separated and needed to go and change into an outfit provided upstairs. Everyone was really excited and ran up the stairs. We were all wondering what it could be. Some girls thought it would be haute-couture gowns, some guys thought it would be a photoshoot for sportswear. I just hoped it wasn't anything too revealing as again I hadn't tanned my legs.

Myself and the remaining boys walked into our room. There was a hamper in the middle with a set of instructions perched on top of it. 'Dear contestants, congratulations for making the cut. Over the course of this weekend you will be whittled down to twelve. If you are successful, you will move into the contestant house and fight for your place. Please change into the briefs required for your first boot-camp challenge.' Briefs? Should that have said 'the brief'? I'm confused.

Jay opens the hamper to find LUMINOUS PINK SPEEDOS. Yep, luminous pink Speedos. My heart just sank. I couldn't believe this was happening to me again. Before I could say 'jazzy pink Speedos', the rest of the guys stripped and put them on, while I ran next door to the girls to see if any of them had some instant tan. Luckily one of them did. As we made our way downstairs we saw the girls had already lined up and were standing in lingerie, while us boys joined them in our pretty pink Speedos. I looked like a prick.

In groups we were asked to go into the ballroom to speak to the judges. My group had Mr Ireland, who walked in first in his bright trunks, eight-pack Jay and . . . well, me. I was holding on to my willy for dear life. You couldn't even see it – it pretty much went inside, to be honest. One by one the judges would ask each of us why we should stay in the competition. When it was my turn I said the following: 'Listen, if you're looking for some ripped muscle Mary, then by all means put these ones through, that's not me. But if you're looking for someone who likes modelling, ain't afraid to say what they think and has fun whilst they're doing it, then take me.' Katie did the same smirk she always did . . .

Over the course of the weekend we were asked to design a clothing brand, do other mini-challenges, but our main job was to impress the judges. I quickly realised by the way the producers and camera crew were behaving that this wasn't just a modelling competition, it felt more like a reality show. Something I knew I was perfect for.

The two nights passed and it came to deliberation day. Only twelve of us would make the cut and move into the contestant house a few weeks later. We all lined up on a grand staircase. One by one the judges would call out names of successful contestants. Melissa, Jemma, Sarah, Kirsten, Susie, Billy, Rehea, Tayla-Jay, Nathan, Jamie, Amy and Raylon. I did it! She still couldn't say my made-up name, but I fucking did it! We all congratulated each other and headed home, knowing that in a few weeks we would all be living together in a house, fighting for a contract.

I packed my case and headed to a hotel in London where all the contestants were meeting up. It reminded me of when I was supposed to be going on *Big Brother*. The London hotel. The production crew. It gave me a right buzz.

Whilst waiting for everything to fall into place, I was standing on the balcony of the hotel with a couple of the contestants. My phone started to ring from a withheld number. I ignored it. It called again. I ignored it . . . again. The third time I answered it. I knew I didn't have long to chat because our phones were being taken off us as we weren't going to be having contact with anyone during our time on the show.

'Hi, is that Rylan?' a voice on the phone asked.

'Yeah, who's this?' I asked in my butchest voice, thinking it was a prank phone call.

'Hi, Rylan. My name is Emma and I'm calling from *The X Factor*. I'm just calling to congratulate you because your audition tape was successful and we would like to invite you to come and audition.'

Fuck, I applied for *The X Factor*? I quickly remembered that I'd sent in a drunk video a few months back. I didn't know what to say – it was *The X Factor*. One of the biggest shows on TV. But I'd literally just signed the contract for *Signed by Katie Price*. 'I'm so sorry but I won't be able to come,' I said. I then went on to explain that I was taking part in another show.

'That's a shame, Rylan. Well, if you're interested in appearing next year, we're happy to keep your details on file . . .'

'OK,' I replied, and hung up. I couldn't believe it. I was standing there with two shows interested in me – it's like those bloody buses, for fuck's sake. I gave the producers my phone for safekeeping and thought no more of it.

Back on *Signed by Katie Price*, we were finally taken to the house where we would be living and filming. It was a beautiful six-bedroom mansion in Roehampton, London. It was round about May and it was quite hot. There was a Jacuzzi in the garden and all the mod cons you could want. As soon as we saw the Jacuzzi we stripped and hopped in. To my amazement there was a pole in the living room – I couldn't wait to get on and entertain the rest of the gang. We all got on so well; it felt very familiar, like we'd all known each other for years.

Over the following weeks the competition heated up, as challenges always resulted in one person leaving the competition for good and moving out of the house. It was like a cross between *Britain's Next Top Model* and *The Apprentice*. It was all pre-recorded and was due to go out later in the year on Sky Living. Some of the challenges were hilarious. One of them was to film a video to upload to YouTube and for it to get the most hits. We were put into groups of three. I was in a group with Melissa and Jemma. Melissa was your typical beautiful blonde model type from Liverpool, and Jemma was a tattooed, fierce-looking glamour girl.

We decided to film some random video where Jemma was in a sumo suit standing by a lake, and I was dressed in a skin-tight onesie and I was meant to push her in. It was literally a nothing video. It didn't mean anything or do anything but, come on, isn't that what most viral videos are viral for? We finished filming and headed back to the contestant house. Jemma was soaking and smelt like duck shit mixed with general pond aromas. Gawd bless her. To make sure we got views, we decided that for the second part of the challenge we would go around London handing out leaflets to promote it. The girls wore bikinis; and I of course wore the dashing neon pink Speedos with a metal jacket. Genuinely. I remember standing in the middle of Oxford Circus, willy pretty much on show, dolled up to the eyeballs, screaming at random passers-by to watch our 'sumo push her in the pond' video. It was a really weird set of challenges but none of us cared. We were on TV and we all thought the show was going to be massive.

One of the last challenges was the 're-style challenge' where we were all taken to the Vidal Sassoon salon in Mayfair and given a makeover. Some of the girls had their hair cut short, a few had a colour change . . . I was made to have my hair cut short, platinum blond, eyebrows made blond and my beard shaved off. I looked awful, I looked like Gollum. It really hit me, throughout the whole process: the little pasty ginger kid had come shining through, and I felt awful. I've always had a problem with my image, massively. I'm not self-confident at the best of times, as much as I make out to be. This goes back to growing up and being the odd one out – the one who didn't have the right hair colour, the one who had to wear a T-shirt in the swimming pool on holiday. I hate the way I look, which is why I try so hard. But this time I couldn't fight it. I thought by now I had buried all that shit, learned not to be so concerned about image, but deep down I knew it would always be a problem. I hated what I could see in the mirror. I broke down. The show completely broke me at that point and I wanted to leave. The following day I nearly did.

We had to do a photoshoot with our new looks with a top photographer. I didn't want to be there. I didn't want to do this anymore – my confidence levels were below the basement. After a lot of persuasion I agreed to carry on. I also got it agreed that my eyebrows would at least be dyed back to black. I did the shoot and, I can't deny it, the results looked striking. But I still hated my looks and with each passing day in the competition I felt more and more defeated. Thank fuck there were members of the public who were brought in to give their opinions of us. The whole point of the show was for Katie Price to find her next protégé to become a star and model and become a brand. It was important to see and hear what the public thought of us. After all, they were the ones who would be buying into us. This was quite a big one – and easily the most nerve-wracking.

The final five of us walked in one by one as the members of the public were shown a video of our journey on the competition. They were cut-throat, proper slagging each contestant off. I was last to go. Shitting myself, clearly. It all seems a bit of a blur now, but I just remember sobbing. They were so complimentary of me. They said I was the most likeable, the most fun and the most genuine. I was gobsmacked. It meant so much. That's what I've been seeking all my life. For people to look at me and think, You know what, he's all right. Behind the make-up and the white-blond hair, he's a nice bloke and I'm interested in him. It really brought me up from the shit makeover I was given.

I made it to the final three alongside Amy and Kirsten. Amy was a posh-talking eighteen-year-old who was absolutely stunning and looked like a young Cindy Crawford. Kirsten was a stunning blonde girl, who was a bit of a ladette at times but still quite girly. The challenge for us three was to sit down one on one with Katie at her house and literally talk. Talk about why we should be in the final two and deserved to get signed. I stood there in the entrance to Katie's house. It was like a palace – it had an indoor pool, a grand staircase, the lot. I couldn't believe where I was. One by one we waited and went for our talk. I remember walking in the room to see Katie. She was sat with her legs up on her sofa, all casual, and we began to chat. She mentioned that I was the only boy left and asked – because girls sell better – what I could bring to her. I didn't know. 'All I can bring is me,' was all I could reply. We spoke about the focus group and how they liked me, and I could see she was really impressed by that. The day before, we'd all had to do a one-on-one shoot with Katie. She gushed at how similar we both were in the fact that we got the right shot of us together in under forty seconds, while the other two took quite a while. We also had to do an individual shoot of us promoting a perfume we'd designed, which was to be released if you won the competition. She pulled out the image of the both of us for us to see for the first time. I was shocked. It was amazing. We looked like brother and sister. Finally she pulled out the picture of the fragrance I had designed. Rylan: ID – Be Who You Wanna Be. She loved it. I was the only one who did a uni-sex fragrance.

Our chat went well and at the end we kissed and had a cuddle. I left. At this penultimate point of the competition, talking things through with Katie really made me feel secure. Not in the sense of competing, but in the sense that I had achieved what I set out to achieve.

Acceptance; the feeling that someone who I've looked up to and admired for years got who I was. Katie understood, and that was more important to me than winning. If it was now my time to leave the show, I could leave with my head held high.

I was put in a car with Amy but without Kirsten. We were told that Katie had already made her decision and that we were her final two; the only ones going back to the house. I couldn't believe it. I was elated. We both had a little cry in the car and went back to the house to get ready for the final day of the competition. I awoke the following morning knowing that it was all coming to an end, but potentially that it could also be the start of a whole different rest of my life.

Myself and Amy arrived at Café de Paris in Central London. The whole place was kitted out with rows and rows of seats and a stage. The final assignment was to present our fragrance to an audience of friends and family and *real-life press*. It was so nerve-wracking knowing, for the first time throughout this whole experience, that we were to be judged by the actual press. The same people that put Katie where she is today. It was all a blur. Amy looked absolutely beautiful, stunning, she really did, and did a great job with her presentation too. As I stood at the top of the stairs ready to walk down, Katie looked at me. This time the look was different, not the usual smirk. This time it was a look that I could read and one that I interpreted to mean 'I want you to win this but I can't let you win this.' I had heard whispers all series that originally the whole competition was only going to be open to girls, because the kind of work that had been lined up for the winner beforehand was mainly female-orientated. I knew all I could do was give it my best, and that I did.

I walked down the stairs to the stage wearing a space-man silver fur-lined jacket, matching boots, with four half-naked models in tow. I pitched Rylan: ID like it was the best-selling fragrance in the world, and when asked questions by the press I had an answer for everything. There was no more I could do. As I waited for the result I knew what had to happen. As much as I wanted to win the show, part of me always knew I couldn't. I was ready. As myself and Amy took to the stage, Katie walked out. She started to get upset. It was strange – I'd never seen Katie Price cry before. As she was trying to announce the winner, she really couldn't hold back and she completely broke down in floods of tears. It was so hard to watch. I took her hand, knowing that it was my turn to comfort her and gave her the same smirk she had been comforting me with for the past month. She smiled. As she wiped away her tears she announced that the winner of *Signed by Katie Price* was Amy.

I wasn't upset, in fact I was happy for Amy more than anything. This was an eighteen-year-old girl with the world at her feet and I was genuinely chuffed for her. Katie came straight over to me and gave me the biggest hug ever. She whispered in my ear that she was sorry and that it wasn't the end for me and her. I knew it wasn't.

After a few months being back home, *Signed by Katie Price* was due to start on TV. Whilst I was away my friends Lucy and Charley had auditioned for *The X Factor* and had made it to judges' houses! I was so over the moon for them, and was glad to see that all our hard work had paid off and it was all happening for us at the same time. However, as *Signed by Katie Price* started airing on TV I instantly knew it wasn't a major success. Viewing figures were low and it wasn't making the impact that the channel had hoped it would, which was such a blow as I really thought this would my big break. Meanwhile, over on *X Factor* the girls changed their name from New Shoes to 2Shoes and made it to the live shows. There was no way I was going to miss their performance but as I made my way to the *X Factor* studios I couldn't help thinking . . . What if? What if I had said yes to the call from *The X Factor* and had gone for that instead? Would I be the one standing here? It bothered me slightly because early showings suggested *Signed by Katie Price* wasn't the runaway success it was meant to be. I feared it would all be for nothing,

I wasn't going to let that ruin my support and excitement for the girls though. I cheered, cried with joy, and screamed their names the whole way through the show, even though, at one point during her energetic rendition of 'Something Kinda Ooooh' Lucy had half a tube of lipstick smeared across her face because the mic had rubbed her lips. At the end of the show we went into the studio bar to see them. They were brilliant and I told them so. As we were leaving, Gary Barlow was walking along the corridor towards us. The girls said hello and introduced me and Lucy's mum to him. He shook my hand and asked if he'd met me before. I didn't really know what to say. It's Gary fucking Barlow! 'I don't think so,' I replied, shared a little laugh with him and left. Just you wait, Gary Barlow. We'll be seeing a *lot* more of each other very soon.

'It was #nerve-wrack'

Rylan Ross Clark 2012

9

The girls were eliminated from the competition, which was gutting for all of us, but I had a feeling that they would be just fine on the outside. They were hard-working and talented. Before too long they were gigging all over the country and loving life – that's sometimes all you need. I went to a few of their gigs and was introduced to their tour manager. His name was Ben, a lovely bloke, also from Essex. Straight away I said to him, 'If one day I ever need a tour manager, I'm going to choose you.' He looked at me as if to say, Yeah all right mate, like that's going to happen. We had a good laugh while the girls were on stage. I said to him, 'Don't underestimate me. I'm a man of my word, and if I do well in life, I'll choose you.' He looked after the girls well, and I knew I'd be in good hands – why wouldn't I choose him? It became our long-running joke over the following weeks and the girls thought it was hilarious.

Back in my world, *Signed by Katie Price* was still on the downhill ratings slope and wasn't getting the views it should have done. I do feel that the show wasn't promoted as much as we expected it to be, and lots of people didn't even realise it was on TV without being told about it. By me. I remember having a phone conversation with Katie mid-series, and she even said herself how disappointing it was. When the star of the show knows it's not doing great for them, as a supporting artist you know you're not going to get much from it.

As the final episode aired and Amy's victory was announced on TV, it was all systems go in the press to welcome a new star to its headlines. I saw in the papers there was a lavish press conference with Amy and Katie, a black Range Rover was given to her as part of her prize for winning, as well as a contract to be signed to Katie's management company.

I was jealous, of course I was. I had kept in touch with Katie and she'd quickly become one of my closest friends. But I didn't feel the need to bring it up with her. One, because I was still annoyed that a girl had won the show, and two, I felt like I could trust her. I ended up going back to work at my friend Helen's studio photoshopping. As much as I enjoyed it, it was just like when I was supposed to go on *Big Brother*, thinking it would be the start of my new life, only to return deflated.

The months passed and 2Shoes were doing great with their gigging and had released a single. In other news, Amy sold a story on Katie saying she was misled and mistreated. Instantly this defaulted her contract, just to put the final nail in *Signed by Katie Price*. It wasn't all lost, because I got Katie as a friend out of it, which was worth more to me. Not because of who she is, but for *who* she is – a normal, down-to-earth girl I could trust and have fun with. I think it was safe to say that the show wouldn't be returning for a second series.

April 2012 soon approached. I was still working in the studio. I had had a call from an old friend who wanted to set me up on a blind date. I was single and desperate so I agreed to it. One Thursday evening I was round Helen's and my not-so-blind (I blatantly checked him out on Twitter) date arrived to take me out for a meal. His name was Mr F. Good-looking, had a nice car, good job, everything seemed great. After a really nice meal out we headed back to Helen's for a little drink. He very much seemed like what I was looking for. Polite, at times sarcastic, but always funny with it. It had gone well. We started seeing each other, and over the following few weeks we went out for meals, or we would just meet up and chat for hours. I knew that I'd started to *really* like this bloke – and when I say really, I mean I can see this being something really proper. That's when I found out he had a boyfriend. ERM, YES . . . BOMBSHELL. The reason I've just casually dropped that line into this book like that is because that's exactly how it hit me in real life. OUT OF THE FUCKING BLUE! He was with someone, and had been for a few years. It was so strange, everything was going so well and then that comes to the table.

We didn't see much of each other after that. I certainly didn't want to be involved in it all but I really did like him. It was such a shame. Men are bollocks. A week after this drama, my mobile rang. It was a withheld number. As usual I ignored it. After a few more calls, which I didn't answer, I got a voicemail. 'Hi, Rylan. My name is Emma and I'm calling from *The X Factor*. We spoke last year when you submitted your application and you said you were interested in auditioning. Please give me a call back.' Oh God, was this yet another thing to get excited about only for it to all fuck up? Why am I bothering? For the last however many years, all I've done is try, work hard, put myself out there, just to be shot down even when I've done it well. I decided not to call her back. I didn't want to be known for jumping from ship to ship in a desperate bid to get to where I wanted to be – it was muggy. I was starting to feel like a 'reality reject'.

A few weeks on and I was still working at the studio. I had fun there, don't get me wrong, but the voicemail kept playing on my mind. I didn't want to call her back, but deep down, my will to succeed and show the world who I am was too strong. I walked outside and made the call. She was lovely – warm, friendly. I had nothing to lose, *literally nothing*. I was given an audition date and told to arrive at 7 a.m. at the O2. Seven a.m.?! Surely she's taking the piss . . . She wasn't.

A week before my audition I was booked to do a modelling job over in Ibiza. Only a small job but whilst I was out there I was desperate to see my mates. I went with Lucy and Tracey. After the shoot, I had a full head of

THE LIFE OF RYLAN

white blond men's hair extensions in. I looked like the lion from *The Wizard of Oz*'s gay brother. I decided not to have the extensions taken out as I knew if I turned up to my audition looking like I did, I'd have more chance of 'making the cut', shall we say. As much as it's a singing show, I knew I wasn't the strongest. I can sing (as much as everyone doesn't think I can), but I knew it was also an ENTERTAINMENT show. The extensions were staying!

Whilst we were out in Ibiza, myself, Lucy and Tracey went to a place called Es Vedrà. Es Vedrà is a small rocky island located about a mile off the mainland of Ibiza. I'd never been whilst I was in the boy band but I'd heard of it. As I drove down a steep decline into a small bay, I finally saw it. It was stunning. A rocky mountain-type island with a smaller one next to it out in the middle of the shimmering ocean. Instantly I knew why people went there. There was something about it that seemed . . . magical. Legend has it that people would travel to Es Vedrà to make their wishes, as it is supposed to be one of the most magnetic places on earth.

As I parked the car and made my way to the shore there was an eerie silence, like time had stopped. No noise, not even the noise of the shallow waves hitting my feet as I strolled along the beach. The three of us each picked up two pebbles from the beach. Lucy told me to hold them both in my hand, make my wish silently to myself, throw one stone out into the sea and keep the other one with me. As I stood looking out to the island I felt like, for the first time in my life, I was supposed to be there. Right there, nowhere else but there. I silently made my wish. I have never told anyone this. For the first time ever I can reveal that first I wished for my family and friends to be well. I wished that one day I would find someone who would love me as much as I could love them. And finally I wished that I would make it to *The X Factor* live shows to get that stepping stone I need.

I threw one of my pebbles out to sea, and clasped the other for dear life, really hoping that it would bring me the luck I've always wanted. After about half an hour we decided to venture back to where we were staying. As I got into the car and turned on the ignition, the petrol gauge went straight up to a full tank. I know we only had about a quarter of a tank left, as I was looking for a petrol station en route to Es Vedrà. I don't know if it was the magnetism, or the magic, but we returned that car three days later to the hire company, with a full tank of petrol that none of us had anything to do with, courtesy of Es Vedrà. Not a bad start, eh . . . ?

Back home, the eve of my *X Factor* audition had arrived. I was winding myself up *constantly* about why I was even going. I wasn't going to get through. Why am I doing this to myself? If I wanted half a chance, I knew I had to stand out. I had the long blond fake hair, teamed with a pair of fully crystallised Converse Hi-Tops. I don't do things by halves – if I'm going to do a job, I'm going to do it properly.

I didn't sleep at all that night. The sheer severity of the situation was filling me with fear. Look what this show had done for the girls – they were earning money, enough to buy their own places. This could do the same for me. I think all in all I slept for around forty-five minutes before I needed to wake up, wash and blow-dry the weave I was sporting on my head. By 6 a.m. I was dolled up to the eyeballs. I got into my car and made the forty-minute drive to the O2. I met Lee from 'The Essex Factor', Tracey, James, Michelle and our friend Claire at the main entrance. The sun was shining and – weirdly for this country – it was a really hot day. As we followed signs leading us to the audition queue, it seemed quite quiet. There weren't many people walking around the circumference of the dome. We all thought we were in for a right result as we must have been one of the first gaggles to arrive.

We couldn't have been more wrong. As we finally made it round to the other side we were faced with a sea of around 5,000 hopefuls practising singing, high kicks, and one guy even a bit of martial arts . . . It's not *Britain's Got Talent*, mate . . .

After hours and hours of waiting , a lengthy signing-in process was followed by a headshot being taken, short on-camera interviews, and more waiting in line. By 2 p.m. I felt wasted. My ginger skin was roasting under the make-up and tan I had slapped on. Finally, at around 4 p.m., I was taken into the backstage part of the arena. I looked like I was on *The X Factor* . . . which I kept forgetting I was. People sat on silver camera cases, primping and priming themselves in front of two-way camera mirrors. One by one people were being taken on to the stage to almighty sounds of applause and boos. It was #nerve-wrack. My time had finally come. Ten hours after I had first arrived all fresh faced and dandy. Now I was sunburnt and I looked like a bad part-time drag queen.

Dermot was on hand to settle my nerves. He was everything you'd want him to be. Kind, warm, friendly and, INDEED, he does give the best cuddles. A man wearing a headset placed me on the side of the stage – using his fingers as markers, he did the famous *X Factor* countdown. Three . . . two . . . one: off you go. As I walked out on to the stage, all I now remember is the feeling of weight being lifted off my shoulders.

This was it, I was finally here, standing in the place that Lucy and Charley had stood a year before. It wasn't life or death – it could potentially be life-changing, but live for the moment and do it.

The audition was eventful. I made jokes with the judges and went to town singing an Ibiza version of 'Kissing You' by *Romeo+Juliet* . . . as you do. My mind was a total blur and I remember sounding like a washed-up cat that had been put through a mangle, but all the while I was just genuinely loving life, and proper going to town. The strut, the hair flick and the sass. Rita Ora was a guest judge at my very first audition, and she was the first person to give me a yes. Louis was quick to back her up. Gary Barlow soon followed, however this time the response was 'Love your personality, hate your voice – it's a no from me.' Bollocks, that's it, I thought. I felt like it was over before it had even begun.

Tulisa was the last person to give her vote. If no, I'd be straight back to the studio and that would be it, no more attempts, I'd be done. If yes, I'm off to boot camp. She took her time. I felt like I was watching an episode of *The X Factor*, let alone being on it. In my head I could even hear background music building up to the decision. 'I'm gonna say . . . YES!' she finally exclaimed. CUE 'AIN'T NO MOUNTAIN HIGH ENOUGH' BLARING IN MY BRAIN. *I'd done it!* Three yeses! I was over the moon. I skipped off the stage feeling like Mickey Mouse on pills. I couldn't believe it.

That evening, I went home to my mum's to share the news. She was ecstatic. I called my nan and she was so proud. I only told my close family and friends. It was only the first part of the process, but after spending the day there and seeing that so many people didn't make it through, I felt like I'd achieved something.

I waited about two months and during that time Mr F got in touch. He told me that he had split with his partner and that he wanted to see me. Part of me didn't want to, but a bigger part of me did. I agreed to see him. One night after work he met me in Shoreditch and we went to dinner. It felt like it did in the beginning, a clean, fresh start. I wanted to tell him about *The X Factor* but I held back. He didn't really know me as that person. He just knew me as me. Normal bloke, normal clothes, normal hair. I wanted to keep it that way and we started dating again.

Soon enough it was time to pack up my old kit bag and head to boot camp. The long blond locks had been removed and I was sporting short black hair. This year it was being held at the Liverpool arena. I'd never been to Liverpool so it was quite exciting – I mean, come on, the home of Cilla, guys! Before I went, I decided to tell Mr F about it all. He was really supportive and wished me luck. Two other friends of mine had also made it to boot camp – I'd met both of them on 'The Essex Factor'. Mitch, and the girl I placed second to, Aiesha. Both were amazing singers and we decided to travel together on the train. As we arrived in Liverpool, we exited the station to be greeted by a 100-foot wide advertising screen with the words 'WELCOME TO BOOT CAMP' illuminated across it. It felt amazing.

We were taken by coaches to an old church that had

been converted into a bar/restaurant for a pre-party. Everyone had a couple of drinks and was having a little dance. After an hour or so, a special guest was announced, and out walked JLS on stage to welcome us to boot camp and sing a few songs. It was like a private concert. Everyone was on a massive high. After the boys had finished performing, an announcement was made. We were told that the judges had made a vital decision and we were needed in the arena immediately. HOLD UP, I didn't think we were needed until the following day. Believe it or not, I was wearing a onesie and silver UGG boots. No word of a lie. It didn't bother me that I was wearing this when I was just with all the other hopefuls, but there was no way I was going on stage in front of the judges looking like this. I'd planned to return with a brand-new look – Was Barbie, now Ken – that sort of thing. But there was no time to change.

We were rushed out to coaches and before we knew it were standing on stage in an empty Liverpool arena. The judges walked out and took their seats. This time they were joined by Nicole Scherzinger who had signed up to be a permanent judge. Tulisa took the mic. 'Hi, guys. We have been having a chat this morning and unfortunately we believe we have put too many of you through.' My heart sank. Don't tell me I've travelled all the way to Liverpool wearing a onesie and silver UGG boots for nothing.

Everyone's mood completely changed. We'd all been on such a high from the pre-party that no one knew where to look. One by one the judges called out names of contestants who were still going to remain in the competition. If your name was called you were to make your way off the stage, through the arena, and into a holding room where the first challenge would begin. So many names were being called, but not mine. I felt like the biggest prick in the world. After about ten minutes of names slowly being called, finally Tulisa said the made-up one I had chosen for myself, 'Rylan Clark.' I felt amazing – for all of three seconds, because as I made my victory walk past the judges' table I remembered what the fuck I was wearing. Nicole gave me a little smile and Gary looked at me like I'd pissed in his drink. The shame.

Finally I was reunited with Mitch and Aiesha who'd also made it through. Once the final few of us filtered in, challenge one was set to begin. We were put into groups of three and had that evening to work together to sing a song to be performed the following morning. I was paired with two guys, Ottavio and Gathan. It was extremely clear from the start why we were chosen as a unit. Ottavio was extremely extrovert, he was wearing as much if not more make-up than me, and Gathan was an extremely self-assured type of guy wearing a tight white vest. One thing I can't stand is when someone is so self-confident they completely love themselves. Gathan seemed like that type of guy. We instantly clashed, we argued, and he clearly thought he was better than myself and Ottavio put together. Whilst all the other groups were rehearsing, we were arguing. We all thought we knew what was best for the group, but none of us even dreamt of listening to one another, so we just clashed immediately. To make matters worse we were put in the same hotel room together to spend the night. I think we finally ended up getting to sleep around 4 a.m.

After a night of arguing and no sleep we were back in the arena for 9 a.m. As the day went on, groups were performing, and one or two of them from each group were being eliminated on the spot. Mitch and Aiesha had made it through to the next part earlier in the day, which added a bit of pressure. I didn't want to be the one of us

146

who didn't get through. Our time finally came to perform. The song we were given was 'Respect' by Aretha Franklin . . . you couldn't make it up. As I walked out on to the stage wearing a custom T-shirt I'd made from black hair extensions, I knew I wasn't in the mood to take the previous night's shit lying down.

We were asked how rehearsals had gone, etc., by the judges. All of us had no problem saying that we didn't get along and it was a complete nightmare. We were then asked to sing – what Nicole aptly named a 'diva hoedown' then ensued. Ottavio did his best Mariah Carey impression and even walked the width of the stage flicking his hair back – and it was only around two inches long. Gathan channelled his inner Craig David/Michael Jackson mash-up persona and went to town grabbing his crotch and throwing hand gestures like he was having a fit. And there I was stood, hair-extensioned shoulder pads ready, and I looked the most butch out of the three of us.

The judges deliberated. I had no idea what was going through their heads or what was about to happen. Had I done enough? Surely they wouldn't put Gathan through? He seemed a bit of a dick. The judges were finally ready to pass judgement. Tulisa started to speak. 'Gathan and Ottavio, please step forward.' The fact my name wasn't called frightened me. If they went through, I was definitely going home. 'Congratulations, boys, we'd like to see you tomorrow.' I felt like I'd let myself down more than a lilo. I couldn't believe it. The boys exited stage right feeling like they had won the lottery.

'Rylan, please step forward,' Tulisa sombrely mumbled. I just hoped at that point they would send me home nicely and not criticise me or mug me off. 'Rylan, we would like to see you tomorrow.' I froze. 'WHAT?' I shouted. No full group had gone through previously. 'YOU'RE ILL!' I randomly exclaimed. My head was all over the shop. I'd done it! I was through to the next and final part of boot camp. As I scurried off the stage Nicole was putting her thumbs up and smiling at me . . . Something that didn't make the TV edit was the following thing I shouted. As I noticed her clearly showing her happiness I was through, I went to shout out the words 'Pussycat Dolls', but what actually ended up coming out of my mouth still haunts me to this day. I opened my mouth, put my thumbs up towards her and shouted at the top of my voice, 'PUSSSSSAAAAAYYYYYY!' I was mortified. Had I just shouted the word 'pussy' at the top of my voice directly at Nicole Scherzinger's face? Yeah, yeah, I had. Absolute fail.

That evening I went back to the hotel and had a good night's sleep. The following morning I woke up and made the short walk to the arena at 9 a.m. I was wearing zebra-print trousers and a black blazer that I had customised with spikes on the shoulders. This was the final part of boot camp. When I arrived I was told I would be the first person to perform that day. A solo performance in front of 10,000 people. No pressure then. I geared myself up and at 11 a.m. I took to the stage. I performed 'Don't Cha' by the Pussycat Dolls, as I was so embarrassed at screaming at Nicole the night before and so had a bit of grovelling to do. I had fun and the audience liked it. I walked off the stage and ran through the crowds to make my way to Dermot. As I leaned in and wrapped my arms around him to receive one of his trademark cuddles, I heard him shriek. One of the spikes on my blazer had literally jabbed him in the eye. I mean, can you believe my luck? First I shout 'pussy' at a judge, now I've blinded the presenter. He didn't die, that was the main thing.

I was the first to arrive back at the hotel. I got changed and went and sat in the bar. Slowly, throughout the day, contestants would filter back and would join us in the bar. I had been drinking since midday. As the final few contestants started to arrive at the bar at 11 p.m., I was well and truly pissed. Everyone had a good drink that night. I changed into my trademark onesie and UGG boots and partied hard. I went out for a cigarette at about 1 a.m. and a lady came up to me. She said, 'You were really good today and you should be proud of yourself.' Instantly I presumed she worked on *The X Factor,* as the hotel had been taken over by the show. I was so embarrassed that I didn't recognise her or remember her name, so I avoided any further embarrassment by inviting her to the bar. I used my key card to walk her in.

Just as we arrived in the bar, I asked her coyly, 'Sorry, babe, I've had a drink, I can't remember your name.'

'Halina,' she replied.

I walked us both into the bar and at the top of my voice exclaimed, *'Look, everyone, it's Halina!'*

Everyone – clearly wanting to impress anyone that worked on the show – all started chanting, 'HALINA, HALINA, HALINA.'

I left her to her own devices and continued to party. About an hour later I felt someone grab the back of my onesie and pull me into the corridor. It was Russell – he worked on the show dealing with press and publicity. 'Did you bring that woman in here?' he asked angrily.

Pissed up and thinking he must be too, I confidently replied, 'That's Halina,' confused as to why he didn't know who she was.

He just looked at me with his best death stare. 'She's a journalist for the *Sunday Mirror* and she's been taking photos all night of you lot pissed up in here!'

My mouth dropped to the floor. I couldn't believe it. In my drunken state I've walked a journo into our hotel. He was fuming. That was it, I'd made the ultimate fail.

He told me to go to bed and he would deal with it. I sheepishly made my way to the lift and got in. About twenty minutes later I was found passed out in the lift, wearing nothing but my silver UGG boots. One of the contestants helped me to my room and put me to bed. WHAT A STATE. The following morning it was decision time. I felt like I had been run over by a 747 and then repeatedly punched in the face by Mike Tyson. I was hangover as fuck. I bumped into Ella early that morning on our walk over to the arena and we laughed about the previous night's shenanigans. She was a lovely girl and I thanked her for helping me in my hour of need.

We all arrived back at the arena the next day and were split into four different categories: boys, girls, groups and over-28s. Group by group we were taken on to the stage to reveal the six people from each category who would be going to judges' houses. The girls were first. Ella sailed through. The groups were next, followed by the over-28s. Finally it was time for the boys. I made my way up to the stage with the remaining nineteen boys. I felt sick, mostly because of nerves, but the hang-over didn't fucking help. The judges took it in turns to announce the names of boys who were through to judges' houses. Jake Quickenden, Adam Burridge, James Arthur, Jahméne Douglas, Nathan Fagan-Gayle . . . At this point Gary was handed a card, he looked at it, he passed the mic and the card to Louis and said, 'You'd better read this one . . .' Louis then literally pushed me over the edge . . . 'RYLAN CLARK . . .'

I fell to the floor; I couldn't look anyone in the eye, mainly because of my blurred alcohol vision, and stumbled off the stage to Dermot. I couldn't actually speak, not taking the piss – I COULDN'T ACTUALLY SPEAK. I don't know if it was the cosmopolitans the night before or the sheer shock, but I'd done it. I'd made it to judges' houses! I joined the five other boys in the holding room and we all had a good chat. James, Jahméne and Nathan were quite quiet but I instantly hit it off with Jake and Adam. Unfortunately Mitch and Aiesha didn't get through – I couldn't believe that out of our little group, I was the only one who made it. We were all brought together with the other categories that made it through. Happy and relieved we all congratulated one another.

The following day was my mum's surprise sixtieth birthday party that myself and my brother had planned. It turned into a double celebration for us all. It was held in a large ballroom in a hotel in Essex and I had even arranged for a professional photographer to come and set up a studio area because my mum always complained she didn't have any nice photos of her and her friends. Well, there you go, Linda, now's your chance. We had such a great night, apart from when I ripped the arse out of my trousers from slut dropping. Standard Essex party etiquette.

RYLAN CLARK-NEAL

All my close friends were there – James, Katy, etc. Even Mr F made the effort. It was the first time he had been in a room with all my family. It finally felt like I was in a relationship that was normal and all my family and friends knew about it. The thing was, we never had the chat about seriousness, we just began dating, but it was more than that. I wasn't seeing anyone else and to my knowledge neither was he, so everything was good.

However, a couple of weeks before judges' houses, things didn't feel right. We would arrange to meet up and most times something would come up and he couldn't make it. I felt like he'd lost interest so I called him out on it. He said that since he had just come out of a long relationship he didn't feel that he wanted to jump straight into another. That upset me. Here we go again, I felt like I was getting messed around. I didn't argue, I just left him to it. We went our separate ways. I had to think about myself. I was at a point where my life could change overnight if I played my cards right. So I didn't fight it. I had bigger things to worry about. If only I knew how big things were about to become.

'When in Dubes.'

Rylan Ross Clark 2012

10

It was finally time to face the *X Factor* judges' houses. It was a sunny Saturday in August when I made my way to the London offices. Reunited with the boys, we had no idea where we were going, when we were going or what judge we would be going with. The show had already started on TV. Jahméne and James's auditions had already been showed and they were amazing, just as they were in real life. I was told that my audition episode would be airing the night we were due to leave, so I wasn't sure I would get to see it as there was a chance we would be on a plane. I was gutted. I needed to know what people thought. How was it edited? Did I look like a prick? I had to forget about it. I had work to do.

I was given the song I was to sing: Rihanna's 'We Found

Love'. A lovely vocal coach called Annabelle worked with me for a few hours in the studio to make sure I was happy with it. I wasn't, but I wasn't going to moan. After the session we were all taken to Heathrow Airport. During the journey we were speculating where we could be going. Maybe it's Tulisa and we're going to Ibiza? Touch, I could double up as a tour guide. Maybe it's Louis and we're going to Ireland? Just my luck . . . None of us knew. Upon arrival we were gathered at the front of Virgin's first-class check-in. I was handed an envelope. We were going to Dubai! Actual Dubai! I hadn't been further than Europe before so this was a big deal.

We checked in and made our way to the lounge. It was 7.50 p.m. and my phone started making noises. Constant notifications were pouring in. It was surreal. My audition had aired. We were literally boarding the plane and I had just enough time to check Twitter. Rylan was the top trend, followed by #nerve-wrack as a close second. I was kindly asked by the cabin crew to turn my phone off and I did. Why was I trending? Do people like me? Do they despise me? I had no idea. At this point the production team confiscated all of our phones anyway, and the flight took off for Dubai.

After a nine-hour trip we arrived at the Jumeirah Zabeel Saray hotel on the Palm Jumeirah in Dubai. I had never ever seen somewhere so beautiful. The walls of the hotel were literally made of gold. We were taken to the hotel's Royal Residences. These houses in the tropical gardens of the hotel had private swimming pools, private beaches and personal butlers, and if we we'd been paying for them the whole experience would have cost us around £3,000 a night. It was stunning. I was placed in a residence with James and Jahméne, whilst Nathan, Jake and Adam had another. I hadn't yet had the chance to connect with James and Jahméne, so was a bit apprehensive but soon enough we started to bond.

The first day was pretty much free time. It was meant to be used for us to rehearse, chill out, catch up on sleep and have a wander. The resort was completely out of this world. The spa even had a winter room that was 5°C and had real snow in it.

After a peaceful day in what seemed like heaven on earth, it was time to get some rest. In the morning we would be finding out who our judge was going to be.

The cars came to collect us and we were taken to the marina next to the Burj Al Arab hotel. Lined up along the marina jetty we were told to wait for our judge's arrival. Soon enough, a yacht pulls into the marina, with Nicole Scherzinger waving from the top deck, looking like the ultimate Bond girl. She looked like a vision. Fucking stunning. We all clapped and cheered and helped her off the yacht and on to the jetty. She then introduced her guest judge . . . none other than Ne-Yo. Actual Ne-Yo. I'm standing in a marina, in Dubai, with Nicole Scherzinger and Ne-Yo. What is my life? They both shared some supportive words and we went back to our residences. We spent the next day in rehearsals with the music and vocal team. I couldn't wait to get to bed that night. The heat was so overwhelming, even at night, and I was truly shattered.

I woke up the next morning raring to go. This was the last step of the process before the live shows. This is what I wished for that magic day on Es Vedrà – would it come true? I had my pebble with me to remind me and placed it in my back left pocket. I decided to go for a casual ensemble. You know the kind: tight black shorts, bare-footed, wearing what can only be described as a Kylie Minogue Jedi outfit. Standard. As it was my time, I walked into a grand room where I was greeted by Nicole and Ne-Yo. Nicole asked me why I'd chosen the outfit to wear. I replied, 'When in Dubes.' They both laughed. They were really encouraging and I felt like Nicole really wanted me to do well. I wasn't the best singer – we all knew that – but she knew I had it in me to perform. I started to sing the chilled-out version of the song I'd been given. I sang. I didn't dance, I just sang. When the song finished, Nicole asked me how I thought it had gone. I sighed and told her I had no idea. And I didn't. I genuinely didn't. I left the room feeling satisfied that – up until now – I'd done everything I possibly could.

By the evening, we had all performed and there was no more any of us could do. Me and the boys decided to have a little party in the residence and ordered a few drinks. A few drinks turned into a small off-licence's worth. We were in the pool, on our private beach; we took full advantage of the hospitality, and partied until 6 a.m. Great night, not such a great morning, because at 8 a.m., a mere two hours after I went to sleep, I was woken up by the production team to start getting ready as the result would be announced in two hours. It was like boot camp all over again. I felt fucked, only this time I was still pissed. I could barely see out of one eye. I felt like I

160

was wearing Gabrielle's eye patch. But could dreams really come true?

I did the best I could to make myself look half present-able and made my way to our holding room. I was outside for no more than thirty seconds when I felt the heat from the Middle Eastern sun melt the make-up directly off my face. I looked a wreck, and felt it too. We were all being held a good 200 metres from where we would eventually get told, so as not to suss who'd gone through or not. As I sat down to wait, I realised I'd left something that I needed. The pebble. I could actually visualise it in my room. I'd left it beside my bed. I asked production if I could go and get it but they refused to let me out. Appar-ently none of us were allowed to leave the room. I remembered from the day before that there were two entrances to the toilets, so I asked if I could go to the men's room. I was escorted to the toilet and went in. I made my way through and out the other door. I ran to my bedroom, grabbed the pebble and made it back within two minutes. Enough time for them to think I had a long wee. Or a little . . . you know.

One by one, each of us would make the nervous walk to hear our fate. The remaining contestants were none the wiser as to how the previous lot had done. Again I was last. All alone I sat in the room staring at the marbled walls and opulent mirrors. I still felt like shit, to the point where if I was told I was going home, which I genuinely thought I was about to be told, it wouldn't bother me. I felt sick, hungover and hot. Going home seemed a much preferable option to this torture. Finally I was escorted to the results room. I just wanted to get it over and done with. Just as I was about to walk in, I see Caroline Flack standing by the door. I gave her that look as if to ask, Am I through? She looked at me all sad and she shook her head as if to say, Sorry babe, not this time. I walked in. The walk to the sofa Nicole was sat on seemed like a mile. In actual fact it was about six metres. I sat down and looked into her eyes. I immediately told her it was OK. Hark at me dishing it out like I'm Sylvia Young, I'm telling *her* it's OK. She started talking. Saying how there were some amazing singers left and she wants to win, etc. Hurry up, I thought, I'm hanging here. I felt ill, tired, and I was sweating. The last thing I remember her saying was the now-famous words that shaped one of reality TV's most talked-about moments. 'It's such a big risk . . . that I have to take . . .' I just died. Right there on the spot. 'Is this a wind-up?!' I said and genuinely thought. I looked around the room to the cameramen, producers, lighting guys, waiting for one of them to tell me it was. I just broke. I was physically broken. It had finally happened. The hangover and heat took over my body and I completely broke down. I couldn't breathe, I couldn't speak. I genuinely think I lost half of my body's water in tears. At one point I ended up UNDERNEATH the sofa. I still don't know how. I reached for whatever I could get my hands on to wipe away my stream of continuous tears. Unfortunately for the hotel it was a $2,500 Versace limited-edition cushion, which by this point was covered in the remaining make-up that hadn't already melted off my face. Now most people remember this moment as it has become so infamous. One thing people don't realise is that this breakdown went on for no less than twenty-three minutes. No one could control me. At one point I think Nicole even asked if there was a paramedic because she thought I was having a fit. Genuine fear covered her face and, after a while, I realised I needed to assure everyone I was just so shocked and not indeed dying on the spot.

I remember thanking her and walking out of the room,

still wailing like a sick child. Dermot received the tail-end of the storm, with me repeatedly screaming that he was out of order for having a poker face, and also with me hitting him around the legs whilst I was crouched down in the foetal position on the floor. All of this took place whilst I was wearing a custom-made jumper – yes, *jumper* – to resemble bats' wings. Of course it was. Once I finally settled down from 100 per cent mental to 80 per cent, I was escorted back to the residences. I didn't even think about who was going to be in there – and with which of the other boys I was about to embark on what would turn out to be the most important journey of my life to date. I walked in and immediately saw Jahméne's face. He smiled and walked over to give me a cuddle. I wept on him for around five minutes. I then spotted that James was there too. He cuddled me as well. I also wept on him for around five minutes. I was upset for the other boys who didn't get through. They were kept in another part of the hotel until later on. I'd grown espe-cially close to Jake and Adam so I was really sorry they were leaving. After a couple of hours of press interviews with James and Jahméne I finally managed to calm down. All done, we were reunited with the other three boys. They were all so cool about the situation and we all had a drink to celebrate the fact that we had all got this far.

The following morning we boarded the flight back to London. When we landed I said goodbye to Jake, Adam and Nathan. Myself, James and Jahméne all shared a little moment, knowing we would be seeing each other very soon, and living together! Something that was never shown on the TV was that my mum, my nephew Harvey and my niece Olivia were waiting at arrivals. I still hadn't told anyone the result as production team still had my phone. As I walked through customs I could see them standing there with these 'Don't worry, we still love you' commiserative smiles going on. I just smiled back as if to confirm their thoughts. As I gave them all a kiss, I started to walk towards the exit. I turned around to them and said, 'By the way, I'm through to live shows.' My mum screamed, Harvey couldn't believe it and Olivia just smiled. They were as shocked as I was, but with fewer tears naturally.

I went home that night and finally turned my phone on. I did the one thing I never should have done. I looked on Twitter. I was getting slated left, right and centre. I watched my audition episode and I could see why. I looked a state, I was dressed like a state and I sounded like a state. People thought I was the joke act and it really bothered me. But I knew something that they didn't – I knew I was through to the live shows. Take that.

A few weeks later boot camp aired on TV and the whole diva hoedown situation played out again, and me nearly blinding Dermot! Seems everyone had an opinion on me, good and bad. I knew I was the joke act. Every series had one. The only difference was I actually knew it, and was under no illusion otherwise. I've always wanted to be a pop star, that much is true, and I can sing, but just standing there and singing on the spot was not going to help me in this competition. There were eleven other people through to live shows who were doing that. I had two options. I could let the negativity stop me from continuing with the show and give that place to someone else, or I could carry on, take it for what it was, and play along with it. I decided on the latter.

However, it wasn't going to be easy. In the gap between judges' houses and moving into the contestant house, my nan had begun to show early signs of dementia. She was still living with my aunt but she started to get argumen-tative. My nan is one of the most caring women you could ever meet, who never once took anything out on anyone. I never really listened when my mum and aunts would tell me that she's getting worse. I used to find it funny. She would say things that made me laugh and went through what I like to call her 'dirty stage', where every bloke she met she flirted with. I found it hilarious. To me she was just getting old. I didn't let it bother me.

The live shows were about to begin, and all finalists were reunited and moved into the contestant house. But something was different, *very* different. This year the contestant house was none other than the five-star Corinthia Hotel near Charing Cross. Previously the contestant house was a genuine house somewhere in North London, away from Central London. We couldn't believe our luck. Me and James were sharing a room. At first I didn't know how that was gonna work, but what I hadn't anticipated is how much of a strong bond we would form in a short space of time. So there we were. Fully fledged *X Factor* finalists. James Arthur, Jahméne Douglas, Ella Henderson, Lucy Spraggan, Jade Ellis, Melanie Masson, Union J, District3, MK1, Carolynne Poole, Kye Sones, Christopher Maloney . . . and me. We all felt like a unit. Over the two weeks leading up to live shows, we all had our makeovers. Jamie Stevens and his team of stylists were there to help us with everything to do with hair. A make-up team to work with us for shoots and shows, a styling team that could have rivalled Kim Kardashian's, a music team to make our custom tracks, and vocal coaches to help us along the way. We had everything and the public had no idea. The show was only up to boot camp. It was so surreal, this all happening around me. The *X Factor* glam shoot, the voiceovers were all made and ready to go. I couldn't wait to hear the words 'RYLAN CLARRRKKK' in Peter Dickson's familiar voice. But not one person from the general public knew we were all set and ready to go.

One of my fondest memories to date was the Sunday before live shows. Myself and the finalists all gathered in our green room at the Corinthia to sit down and watch the reveal on TV, along with the rest of the country. As the episode ended and the secret was finally out, we all just hugged each other and celebrated. That was when it finally felt real. Part of me thought, If I haven't seen it on the telly yet, it might not actually happen. But there it was, my name flashed up on the screen with my glam-shoot VT. We all just looked at each other and thought,

From *Signed by Katie* – We could be sisters!

At Es Vedra making wishes.

The lucky stones.

Where it all began – GO ON THE BLONDE!

Arriving at Bootcamp in Liverpool.

Me, Mummy and Nanny at Mummy's 60th.

Me and my Brother Jamie.

Don't mess with Nanny Rose!

My gorgeous Harvey and Olivia.

Just before judges houses… we were right…

The day my life changed forever.

The first ever picture of the Scherzy boys.

X Factor Finalist

Me and my little sister Ella that day we moved into the Corinthia.

Roomies!

The Nicole lift became quite the thing.

That night…

That Scherzy ain't half flexible.

DYING!

Birthday night out with these two…

Night out gigging, spice up your life.

Spice Up Your Life!

CBB late night fun.

Actually in a bath with Claire from Steps, Kathy Beale and Gina from *Heartbeat*.

CHAMP!

We've done it. I only wish I'd then known that from that evening my life would not be the same again for the foreseeable future and quite possibly never.

The following morning I woke up in my five-star hotel room, my new home for the time being. And the real work was about to begin. We were all taken to 'routining'. This would happen every Monday, Tuesday and Wednesday. Routining was spending time with the music team, vocal coaches, choreographers, dancers, stylists and everyone else involved to pick your song, make your track, work on a vision. Right down to what colour the floor would light up at certain points of your song. No detail was left unattended.

I hadn't managed to see any press, or even look at my Twitter as we were all so busy, but during one lunch break I asked to go to the shop. I was taken out of the rehearsal building we used in Battersea via the front door. So far we'd always use the entrance round the back. As the doors slid open there were about a hundred people gathered outside, including A LOT of photographers. They all started to scream and wave their arms. I had no idea what was going on. I didn't realise that they were screaming because of me. It frightened me. I couldn't process what was going on. It's something that I'd always dreamt of having, and now that it was finally happening, it scared me.

Maybe it's because I didn't know how the public were responding to me, but all that week I felt the press go to town on me. I was being slated in the papers, people were rinsing me on social media; all the more reason to be the photographers' number-one target. It was frustrating to read that all these people, people who hadn't even had a chance to get to know me, were making judgements based on around two minutes' worth of collected footage. It wound me right up. Give me a chance. And the craziest thing of it all was I hadn't even performed yet.

On the Thursday night before the first live show, I was sat in the hotel room alone. I'd taken a break from rehearsing for my first performance. I wanted to go to the shop over the road from the hotel to buy some cigarettes. We weren't allowed to leave the hotel on our own 'for our own safety'. Our entire floor of the hotel was crawling with security. It was like an MI5 mission. I just wanted to feel normal for a second and go to the shop on my own. I knew there were die-hard *X Factor* fans outside the front of the hotel, but I also knew there wasn't anyone round the back, by the catering entrance. I slipped out of my room and walked in the opposite direction to where the security guys were standing. I slid into a service corridor and made my way though the maze of tunnels which finally led me downstairs to the back service entrance. I popped my head out the door and looked both ways. There was no one, not even a pigeon. I put my hood up and walked across busy Charing Cross Road towards the Embankment. I walked into the store and bought my cigarettes like any other person would. As I walked out all I could see were bright white lights. There was a sea of photographers waiting for me. They were relentless. I was blinded by the flashlights and couldn't see a thing. I was on my own and just wanted to get back to the hotel. I tried to make my way across Charing Cross Road whilst trying to hide my face in my hood. Mission almost accomplished. I was walking real fast, trying to get back as soon as I could before they noticed I was gone. I tripped and fell in front of an oncoming car. Thankfully the car swerved on to the opposite side of the road. If the driver had been going that little bit faster, he would have definitely hit me. No doubt about it. I peeled myself up from the ground and scurried back to the service entrance. The whole time a sea of bright lights blocked my way. At no point did any of them stop clicking to help me get up from the road. Instead they waited till I was face down on the ground to get a shot of me lying in the road. I ran to the catering entrance and back up to my room.

No one seemed to notice I had left on my own and, from an *X Factor* point of view, I had got away with it. I went out on to my balcony to have a cigarette, thinking about what had just happened. It really shook me up. I grabbed my iPod, put my earphones in and hit shuffle. One of my favourite tracks started to play. Ian Brown, 'F.E.A.R.' It was then and only then that I really started to listen to the lyrics of that song. One of the main lines resounded in my head and really hit home. It completely summed up how I was feeling at that moment. Ian was singing about finding everything and realising how scared you are when you actually find it. It was so true. I really had found everything I wanted, but I was beginning to become very frightened of it.

The following day was the first time we all went to the *X Factor* studios to rehearse. I walked into the studio and stood on the very stage I had watched for the previous eight years. I looked up to see rows and rows of empty audience seats, thinking back to the time I was sat there the previous year supporting my girls. It felt surreal now I was on the other side

The first live show was upon us. I was singing 'Gold' by Spandau Ballet. It was action stations all round. People with headsets running around all over the place. Nicole was on hand to calm me and the boys' nerves as much as she could. She was always there to talk to. After hours of rehearsals and endless styling, I sat in the make-up room having my face done. I walked out looking like a gay Tutankhamun. As I left the styling department, the Egyptian-inspired make-up was teamed with some black skinny-fit jeans, gold trainers, a gold Chanel belt and a gold metal chainmail vest. Just a casual look for Rylan as per usual. You only get eight audience tickets per show and I had decided that I would give my Saturday tickets to friends and my Sunday tickets to family, logic being that if I was eliminated my family would be there for me. James, Katy, Michelle and the gang had already texted me to say they were in their seats. They had made banners and T-shirts, the lot. For me it was a huge comfort to know that they were there for me, cheering and supporting me on my first night.

The show began and it was all a complete whirlwind.

I remember standing behind the famous screen doors before I was about to go on stage. I wasn't ready. I wasn't ready *at all*. I couldn't believe what I was about to do. I do remember, however, that I had made sure I had my lucky pebble securely in my back left pocket. I don't normally believe in things like that, but it had helped me get this far, and I wasn't going to change my ritual. I made my way on to the stage and took my position on a gold platform that was to be pushed around like a shopping trolley throughout my performance. I heard my name play out across the studio and the music began. I remember nothing of that performance. I'm not going to sit here and lie and say I did. I remember nothing. Before I knew it, I was backstage with Lucy Spraggan, who by now was one of my dearest friends in the competition. She gave me a cuddle and told me how well I did. She was the token lesbian and I was the token gay. Christopher Maloney, Jade Ellis and Jaymi from Union J were all gay, but me and Lucy were the obvious tokens. I don't remember the rest of the night either apart from going backstage to the bar at the end of the show and seeing my friends. They were gushing and going on about how I was the top trend on Twitter and how everyone was talking about my performance. Some for good, but mostly for the wrong reasons. I knew what I'd signed up for though. I was never going to be flavour of the month, was I?

I hung out with them for a few drinks until we had to return to the Corinthia with the rest of the team. As I lay in bed, wishing I could fall asleep because I was so tired, I received a text: 'I know what you're doing and you're doing it well. Very proud of you tonight.' It was from Mr F. As much as he'd messed me around before, it had felt like the most normal thing to happen to me all week. I didn't want to text him back, but I did. I replied with the words 'I miss you.' We texted for about an hour and agreed to somehow meet up in the week. I knew deep down I shouldn't really be getting involved with him again, especially as my head was all over the fucking shop, but I needed something relatively resembling normal to take my mind off all the crazy.

Sunday: the first results show. We were all dreading it. We all practised the group number we were singing together. Everyone's nerves were clearly evident. Maloney was shaking in the corner, Jahméne was saying his Hail Marys – we were all in a state. We lined up on the stage: the time had come. Dermot started reeling off names of the contestants who were through to next week. It was bittersweet. As he read each name I was so happy for them but willing my own to be called at the same time. Down to three. As the final safe name was called out, I felt like I had been hit round the face with a spade. I was in the bottom two with Carolynne. No question, no doubt she was a great singer, absolutely stunning to look at as well. As the show went to an ad break, I was pulled backstage and prepped for the sing-off. I wasn't even listening to a word anyone was saying to me. I went numb. I couldn't believe it was all going to be over before it had barely begun. I thought back to earlier on in the year when I said to myself that all I needed was one live show. One live show and I can make a name for myself like the girls did. But the reality had set in. The girls weren't as busy as they used to be. I wanted more. I trusted my lucky pebble and decided what will be will be.

As I walked out the screen doors on to the stage, I placed my hand on my back left pocket. The pebble wasn't there. In that split second I knew I didn't have it. It was on my bedside table. I forgot to bring it. It completely threw me. I was first up. Dermot said my name and the music began to play. It was 'One Night Only' from the *Dreamgirls* film. I just completely lost it. I couldn't hear the track, I was singing out of tune, I forgot all the words. I couldn't believe this was the way I was going to leave the competition. As the track came to an end, I made my way over to stand next to Dermot for Carolynne's performance. She was flawless. It was a no-brainer. Both of us stood in front of the judges waiting for their verdicts. Gary went first and chose to send me home. Nicole was next, and seeing as she was my mentor, she sent Carolynne home. The audience booed, but she'd done what most people would have done and saved her own. Tulisa was next. We had always gotten on well during the competition, she was always wanting me to do well because she really liked me as a person, but even I knew she had to send me home, which she did. It was just Louis left. If he sent me home I was gone. If he sent Carolynne home it would go to deadlock. After what seemed like an eternity of to-ing and fro-ing, he decided to send it to deadlock. The audience gasped. Gary stood up out of his chair. He was Carolynne's mentor and couldn't believe what was going on. The audience's boos were so vehement, I could feel their breath on my face. Dermot was handed the envelope. I knew I was going, I was hated – look at the audience's reaction – and rightly so. I'd probably be saying the same if I was watching at home. Dermot started proceedings. 'The person with the fewest public votes and therefore leaving the competition is . . . Carolynne.' My heart dropped out of my arsehole. The audience erupted in boos and slurs. Gary stormed off stage. It couldn't have been any worse. At that moment in time I would rather have been booted off. I grabbed Carolynne, and apologised in her ear as quickly as I could before I was sent off the stage. I was crying. I felt responsible. Backstage my family tried to calm me down which somehow they always manage to. We said goodbye and I went back to the hotel. The rest of the contestants were really supportive too. And really looked after me that night. I didn't dare look on social media because I didn't want to confirm to myself what I thought the reaction would be. I went to sleep terrified of what I'd wake up to. I couldn't even begin to imagine what was awaiting me the next day.

'I was the country's most
hated person . . .'

Rylan Ross Clark 2012

11

Monday morning broke and I most certainly felt broken. As I woke up I was wishing away the experience, hoping it was a nightmare that just felt like it could have been real. But it was real. It was 7.30 a.m., James was still asleep in the other bed, I was wide awake. There was a knock on the door. As I opened the door I saw that it was Alanda and Sarah, two of the researchers who had been looking after us all. I'd gotten on so well with the two of them – even in the worst crisis they were brilliant. I had a feeling that I was going to need them. We walked to another room in the Corinthia. It was our green room, which had been kitted out for us to relax in. Then they showed me the papers. I was literally front page of most of the tabloids. 'FIX FACTOR',

'NATIONAL JOKE', etc. I was horrified. I wanted to jump out of the window; at that moment it definitely felt like the easier option. I was utterly distraught.

I knew that I had to eventually check my Twitter and 'face the music', as Peter Dickson would say. When I say the word 'barrage', I don't mean it lightly. I was the country's most hated person just because of what had happened the previous night on a singing competition, and, with all due respect, this was at around the same time as the Jimmy fucking Savile case, so you can imagine how I felt. Insults, piss-takes and – more worrying – death threats. Tweets along the lines of 'I know you're living at the Corinthia hotel. I'm going to kill you when you walk out in the morning . . .' And so on. It was terrifying. After an hour or so, most of the other contestants had woken up and were informed what was going on. I felt lucky they were all on hand to reassure and look after me. I most certainly needed it.

Mondays were vocal coaching, where we would start working on our new songs for the Saturday and we would head over to our rehearsal studios in Battersea. I didn't want to go. I just wanted to go home and forget that I'd even done the show. I couldn't bring myself to answer calls from my friends or family because it would probably tip me over the edge because I knew I'd caused them all this worry. I finally got dressed and made my way down to reception. As I got into the lift with Alanda and Sarah, one of the security boys jumped in. I didn't think anything of it. It wasn't until he told me to get directly in the car and not to stop and talk to anyone or have pictures with people that I realised he was there to make sure no one followed through with their threats. Is this *actually happening* to me? All I've done is go on a singing show, for fuck's sake. How has this happened?

As I walked out of the entrance of the hotel, I couldn't even see. There were so many press flashing their cameras, fans screaming, and passers-by gathering to see what all the fuss was about. As I was bundled into a waiting car, fans of the show were asking for photos. There was one guy in particular who was desperate to get one – as I turned to him he took a selfie and thanked me and looked genuinely grateful. His face looked so familiar, I asked him, 'Do I know you?' I was sure I knew him but I just couldn't place him. He looked at me really shocked and even a little scared and I couldn't understand why. On the drive to the rehearsal studios I went back on

Twitter to have a look at the news stories that were written about me. And that's when it clicked. The guy, who was clearly a fan of the show and genuinely wanted a picture with me, was one of the people who had tweeted me threatening to slit my throat in my sleep. It was him, 100 per cent. That's when I understood first-hand what a 'keyboard warrior' actually was. A scummy, filthy prick who – when in the safety of their own home, behind their online profiles – thinks they're Rocky and can say to people whatever the fuck they want, but in real life are small, childish cowards who would jump out of their skin if you even looked at them twice. It was at that moment I knew I needed to start treating the whole experience like a pantomime. If they say jump, you say, 'How high? If they want to verbally attack you, give it back twice as hard. It's panto, it's a real-life pantomime.

Later that afternoon, I was sat with Ella looking online. The abuse was getting worse and was starting to play on my mind, but like a little sister, she kept reassuring me it was all going to be OK. You know you've hit a rough patch when a sixteen-year-old girl is talking more sense than you.

An hour or so later I was told that my song for that week was 'Gangnam Style'. Are you for fucking real?

'Gangnam Style'? Is this a piss-take? Are you literally wanting me to get stabbed live on television? Why on earth would I want to stand on stage in front of millions of people and sing 'Gangnam Style' when I'm already public enemy number one?! I went upstairs to see what choreography and staging Brian Friedman had planned. I walked into a room with a lit-up catwalk, men dressed as Karl Lagerfelds and women dressed as Anna Wintours, and a few people dressed as pandas. Standard Monday afternoon on *The X Factor* then. I looked at Brian and asked if he was high. He laughed and explained that this week was all about me coming back with a bang and taking it for what it is. A show! It's not life or death, it's a Saturday-night entertainment show. He thought this would probably be my last performance. So did I – as did everyone else, to be fair. I listened to what he had to say and he was right, let's go out with a bang. We camped it up to the max and it was shaping up to look like a spectacular visual treat. After that I went back downstairs into vocal coaching. Annabelle was always there along with my other coach Ian, and the music team from Sony was also there. Simon (Gavo) had a little idea. He suggested that, seeing as I used to be in a Take That tribute band, why don't we have a little dig at Gary Barlow because he was so vocal and wound up that I had got through? I knew I had nothing to lose, so I thought, Fuck it. Let's do it. We decided to start the track with the opening lines of 'Back for Good': Priceless. I went back to the hotel that night feeling a little bit better. Still nervous that someone was going to climb through the window and murder me, but definitely more settled than I'd been that morning.

Throughout the week we continued rehearsing, going to events, filming all day everyday. It was tiring. I couldn't help but keep thinking about all the downsides though. The thought that my family and friends would be out shopping or in a bar, relaxing, and someone somewhere might be slagging me off. It made me feel bad for them. Should I really be putting them through this? With my mum's illness I wasn't too sure she would manage to handle this as well. They were all so supportive and told me to carry on. And I'm so glad I did.

Saturday came and it was show day. People in and out of rehearsals, hair and make-up for hours on end. By show time you're completely knackered but you've still got to go out there and give it your all. We made sure not to rehearse the Gary Barlow bit in case he was watching it somewhere on a live feed in the building, so it was most definitely a one-take wonder.

I was up. My turn to stand behind the famous doors and perform. Lights, camera, action. 'I guess now it's time for me to give up. . . AHHHH, I ain't really singing that, that was just for you, Gary!' The audience screamed with laughter, as did Gary. Nicole was literally dying with hysterics and fist-pumping for her life. For some reason I decided to sing 'Rylan Style' instead of 'Gangnam Style'. It certainly paid off as 'Rylan Style' trended on Twitter into the following day. The producers weren't too happy because I changed the lyrics of the world's most famous song at the time, but oh well, I said I'd go out with a bang. After the show I really felt like I'd had fun and put two fingers up to the arseholes who were slating me. With all due respect, I don't judge them for having an opinion, but my job wasn't to be the singer on *The X Factor*, my job was to be, as Nicole said, the X, Y and Z factor. For the first time all week, that evening I got some proper sleep. I'd done what I needed to do: have some fun and not take it too seriously.

Sunday: it's results day again. Everyone at the studio would come up to me saying how well I'd done and a few even said that they were going to miss me. It was sort of common knowledge, everyone just thought I'd be going home – me especially. I literally lived that day as if it was my last. I knew I would be in the bottom two and I wanted to sound half-decent so I worked with Annie for an hour or so on my exit song and I was ready and raring to go. One of my stylists, Rikki, found me a top to wear for the show, which said 'Leave the Boy Alone', which we all had a giggle about and I knew was the perfect slogan for my exit. The show went live and we were on air.

We performed our group song like The Kids from 'Fame' and prepared ourselves for the reveal of the bottom two. Dermot started proceedings in his ever-so-tense manner, leaving gaps of what seemed like twenty-six days between announcing names of contestants through to the following week. James had been called, as had Jahméne, leaving me as the last remaining Scherzy boy on the stage. Nicole was holding my hand and stroking it in the 'I love you, baby, go out with a bang' style. I grabbed my back left pocket to make sure I had my lucky stone on me this time, as I knew it would bring me some good luck for my final performance. Then, out of the blue, it brought me that little bit more luck I didn't think it had in it. 'RYLAN,' Dermot confidently announced. BEND ME BACKWARDS IN A BUSH WITH SEVEN RACOONS LIVING IN IT, IT'S ME! Nicole's face literally dropped, along with my jaw and sanity. I grabbed her around the waist and lifted her into the air, then walked her over to the safe area. I could sense that all the other safe contestants were so made up and genuinely over the moon. Nicole kissed me and whispered in my ear, 'Let's fucking do this, baby.' I couldn't believe it. I was through. The public saved me?! THE PUBLIC SAVED ME!

I was elated. I had so convinced myself I was leaving that I totally wasn't prepared for it. Lucy suggested that we go out and celebrate. We decided to go to G-A-Y Late bar in Soho for a couple of drinks. Throughout the night people were coming up to me, genuinely pleased I was still in the competition. A couple of drinks turned into forty or so, and I was definitely the most drunk I had *ever* been in my life. Once we decided/were informed it was probably best to go back to the hotel at 3 a.m., security from the club escorted the pair of us out to a waiting taxi. Nothing could have prepared me for the crowd out-side. There were what seemed like a sea of paparazzi baying for the picture they knew would sell. The two gays pissed out of their heads. I was so far gone I was fall-ing all over the place, holding on to random person after random person just to move inches along the pavement, which by this point I had fallen on to numerous times. The security guy couldn't find our taxi, so kindly offered to drive us himself to make sure we got back to the hotel safely. We didn't have anyone from production with us, because earlier Lucy and I did a runner to go clubbing. I was bundled into the back of a car and we were taken back to the Corinthia.

When we arrived at the reception entrance it was so late that no one was really outside, apart from these few guys who turned up out of nowhere. I didn't really know what was going on or who they were, but it was eerily quiet. I asked one of them for a cigarette and thanked the security guy for dropping us back. Now you may think, How does he remember all of this if he was so drunk? Well, because it ended up being filmed for an ITN news exclusive by the press who were following us. The guys outside the hotel were in fact photographers. They were casually coercing us into acting up, and us two – being in the clearly drunken states we were – were more than happy to oblige. Lucy pulled my trousers down, they had pictures of my naked arse, *which I would like to add* was a very bad-angled picture. I've got an all right bum. We started to walk to Tesco round the corner as we didn't have any cigarettes – somehow we ended up on a building site falling down holes and throwing traffic cones about. Embarrassing. Watching the video back, which is still online, you can hear the guys filming everything saying, 'Don't make a big scene, keep casual. If no one else gets this on film we'll get £10,000 for this.'

Waking up the following morning, I didn't remember a thing. Late that morning the exec producers of the show sat myself and Lucy down and told us that neither they nor the hotel were too happy about our behaviour last night and that they thought it would be a good idea, to show the hotel we respect their establishment, for us two to move out for a few days into another hotel nearer the studios. Neither of us really wanted to go but it seemed we didn't really have a choice – we didn't want to piss off anyone any further. We were very much under the impression that we would be back a few days later. As you can imagine, this then turned into a big press story. 'RYLAN AND LUCY THROWN OUT OF X FACTOR HOTEL.' As we carried our luggage out of the not-so-glamorous service entrance of the hotel, the press were ready and waiting to capture it all on film. Overnight I'd gone from *X Factor* joke act to *X Factor* bad boy. The shame.

We were taken to another hotel and settled in. Not ones to miss out on anything, we dolled ourselves up and went to an event we had both been invited to that evening. We weren't going to sit in the hotel staring at the wall – this was a once-in-a-lifetime experience and we wanted to embrace everything. As you can imagine, the press loved the fact we were out on the town the very same night we had been evicted from our previous digs. We were young and having fun. I WAS SAVED BY THE PUBLIC! Who knew how long it would last!

Somehow I managed to get through week three after wearing a white jumpsuit with my midriff showing. I certainly wasn't the best, but for some reason the public were keeping me in. The start of week four was my birthday week. Production had organised a birthday party for me at Mahiki in Mayfair. I was allowed to invite my friends and family, everyone from the show was coming – it was going to be a big deal. Me and Lucy were annoyed as we still weren't back living at the Corinthia – it had been over a week now and still no news on when we were to return. Practically we wanted to be more central because it was taking a long time getting to rehearsals and, more importantly, seeing everyone and going out. They decided to move us to a hotel back in Central London for a few nights over my birthday so it would be easier for us to get about. The night of my birthday party arrived. It was fancy dress, and everyone made a massive effort. Even Tulisa rocked up looking amazing in her costume, all dolled up in a sexy French maid's outfit. Nicole had told me earlier in the week that she couldn't make it as she had to fly back to America for a family thing. Once inside the atmosphere was electric. My friends and family were there, all the contestants, the production crew, basically everyone I'd met on this journey and got close to. Then the music went off. Out walked Nicole, dressed like a prostitute devil, singing 'Happy Birthday'. It was amazing. She wanted to surprise me, and she certainly did . . . Along with every man in the club who couldn't believe their eyes at the sight of Nicole in a latex corset. We partied till the early hours and then I made my way back to the hotel we were in for the night.

The following morning I felt rough and even though I'd won the public vote, the threats and taunts I was getting started to break me down. Having to deal with all the abuse and carry on as normal was so hard for me. I had a one-on-one tutor lesson with Robbie Williams – who was lovely and so supportive – but my mind was totally elsewhere. The producers could see how shaken I was and allowed me to go home to my mum's. I had to break the bubble for twenty-four hours to cope with what was an extremely rough time.

Leading up to the Saturday-night show, I was offered the chance to miss the weekend but remain in the competition. Part of me feels I should have taken it; I wasn't in the right frame of mind to go out on stage and be the national joke. I seriously considered it, but I knew if I did it would cause an uproar. I had no choice in my own mind but to carry on. Few people around me knew the reality of what I was going through. It was quite hard keeping up appearances but, like I said, I had to. The show was amazing to me and looked after me during the time as well as they could. Somehow I managed to get through that week and through to week five. The hardest thing was still taking everyone's criticism and insults online, even harder when you're feeling lost and low. But I did it, and I am extremely proud that I did.

Later that week Lucy wasn't well enough to continue in the competition and I was genuinely gutted. She was my best mate on the show, always there for me when I needed her, and living with her away from the rest really cemented our close friendship. Now she was leaving I wasn't too sure how I would cope. Following my break down, I was given an apartment in Westminster for the remainder of my time in the competition. I felt safe, and I felt comfortable there, but the following week I ended up back in the bottom two along with Kye Sones. The judges sent it to deadlock and Kye ended up leaving the competition. I was saved on the public vote. So here we go again, cue the insults.

The best thing that happened to me that horrible week was that my nan was able to come to the show. She had really started to deteriorate and the Alzheimer's was taking over. I'm so proud she was able to see first-hand what I was doing. She was always my biggest supporter and would encourage me to perform, and knowing that she was still aware of what was going on meant the world to me. After the show that evening I was in the bar at the X Factor studios with my nan and the rest of my friends and family when I noticed Jamie East, a presenter from *Big Brother*, over on the other side of the room. As you now know, I'm a massive fan of the show, so I went over to say hi. We spoke for a bit and he whispered something in my ear. 'They want you to do *Celebrity Big Brother* in January.' I nearly collapsed and died on the spot. '*What? What are you going on about?*' I asked him. He gave me a number and asked me to call some woman to discuss it. I couldn't believe what I was hearing. Years ago I was supposed to go into that house and I'd never ever been able to let it go that it hadn't happened, but now I might be going on the CELEBRITY version? Crazy.

I called her that week. A lovely woman named Ros. She was the booker for *Celebrity Big Brother*, and she asked if she could have a meeting with me and my management. I didn't have management before I entered *The X Factor* but I was automatically allocated management when I signed the contract to go on the show. They were lovely guys, but quite highbrow, and I knew they wouldn't let me do *Celebrity Big*

Brother. I said that I would meet her in a restaurant a few doors down from the salon run by Jamie Stevens, our *X Factor* hairdresser, later that day. I was good mates with Jamie and knew he could keep a secret. I called and asked him to tell the *X Factor* production team to put me in a car because he wanted to do my hair. They did it without questioning, and off I went. I popped into the salon and explained the situation to Jamie. He was over the moon, as he'd kept saying I'd be brilliant on it. The public never got to see me off stage, they only get to see the idiot performing in loads of make-up and feathers; this could be my opportunity to show people who I really was. I snuck out of the fire escape of the salon, so as not to get photographed. I went into the restaurant and sat down with Ros. She was lovely, really kind, someone who I'd get on with in general. She basically outright said she wanted me and that was that. I told her I'd do anything to make sure it happened. I needed *Celebrity Big Brother* just as much as she seemed to want me. I left pretty much knowing it was mine if I wanted it, my lifelong dream of being a housemate. A NEW SET OF SUITCASES! But what concerned me was could I actually have it? Would management let me do it? Contractually, was I allowed to do it? So many questions, but I was frightened to ask for answers . . .

Back on *The X Factor*, it was week six and the theme was 'Best of British'. There was no question about what I wanted to perform. THE SPICE GIRLS. After suggesting a megamix of the girls' songs, the music team looked a bit concerned. It had previously been hard to get the rights to perform Spice Girls songs on the show. I didn't give one fuck. I'd been to hell and back on this show, I was singing the Spice Girls and I didn't care if I had to ring Vicky Beckham myself and pipe up. They finally agreed to let me do it. This was MY week. We went all out. I was taken to Norfolk to record jumping out of a plane for the opening of my performance. On the Thursday evening I was asked to do an extra rehearsal. I didn't really understand why, and it wasn't at our normal studio. I was taken to a drama school in North London and was being filmed rehearsing on my own in an empty dance studio. I heard the noise of stilettos walking up the hallway. Then I died.

The End.

'I had to walk over them
without dying.'

Rylan Ross Clark 2012

12

No, seriously, I thought I'd died. GERI FUCKING HALLIWELL WALKS IN! GERI FUCKING HALLIWELL! I WAS HER IN THE PLAYGROUND AT SCHOOL! My absolute idol. Queue more tears than at judges' houses. She was a dreamboat. She was there to help me rehearse and inject a bit of girl power. I was so honoured. Some people might not understand how much of a big deal this was, but to anyone who knows me it was THE DEAL OF THE CENTURY. She was everything I wanted her to be, and more. She was kind, funny, Ginger Spice, and a bit mental, which I loved. She genuinely knew what it was like to keep trying until you succeed – she said she saw a bit of herself in me, and she wasn't going on about my roots. She got me, like I always had got her for the past however many years. She genuinely wanted me to do well. After a few hours of working with her I knew I was more ready than I'd ever be to do the show. We said our goodbyes and I left feeling like the luckiest little ginger kid in the world.

Show day finally arrived. The stage was set and I was ready and raring to go. If this was the last thing I ever did, I'd be a happy man. The choreography was amazing, the dancers were amazing and I even had fireworks. We hit a problem at the top of the performance though: I was being lowered in on a parachute (casual), and one of my friends Aaron, who was a dancer, couldn't un-hook me from my wires. It was touch and go: am I going to be stood here at the back for the entire performance? After what seemed like sixteen hours, he finally set me free and the girl power kicked in and we carried on. It was great. Not the singing, but the whole performance in general was amazing. Nicole was up on the judges' desk, Tulisa was out of her seat, Louis was just pleased to be there, and Gary even cracked a smile. If I'd left at that exact second I would have been over the moon. That's when I started to see the public turn a little bit in favour of me. I think people were finally able to see that, although I wasn't the best, I was having fun with it and taking the piss. I hadn't changed everyone's minds but I knew I had converted some of the public and that was good enough for me. Again, somehow I managed to get through to the following week. Chuffed to bits. That evening my mum came down for the first time. Just like with my nan, it was so lovely for her to be there. For her to be out that long takes a toll, so everyone made a fuss of her and I was so grateful that she managed to see me on the show, not just through a TV screen. After celebrating with my friends and family I was ready . . . Week seven, here I come.

In the January of 2012, before I had even auditioned to go on the show, I went to see a friend of mine, Alex. She's a psychic. She had said to me that I would end up on *The X Factor* and last seven weeks. It was only now that I clocked that she was right and in my head week seven was most definitely going to be my last week. I just wanted to enjoy myself. I was told I was singing a mash-up of 'When Will I Be Famous?' and 'Girls on Film' . . . OK, no problem. I'm just happy to be here. The choreography for it would be on treadmills and set up like a futuristic gym. During rehearsals on show day I didn't realise that the treadmills would be real, switched on, four of them in a line, and I had to walk over them without dying, and singing live. Easy. In the dress run on show day I walked across the first two and my boots caught the grip of the treadmill mat and sent me flying over and dragged me underneath. I guess it would have been sort of all right if it wasn't for the fact that I was wearing a light-up boiler suit with eight battery packs strapped to my bare skin. I was ruined. Cut to shreds, I literally bled through. Only a few hours until show time. I cleaned myself up and carried on. Thankfully I made it over them during the live show and didn't lose a limb in the process. Brucie Bonus.

Gary slated me that night, as he did every week. He asked me who I played in the Take That tribute band I used to be in. I just felt the words bubble up in my throat and I couldn't stop them from coming out. I replied, 'Well, I definitely weren't you, I'm too skinny for that, G.' The crowd erupted. Insult of the series, I thank you. Let's be honest now. There was never any bad blood between me and Gary – maybe week one I took it personally, but from then on we got on well backstage and what happened in the studio stayed in the studio. I've got a hell of a lot of respect for him as a person and an artist. He shook my hand after the show and said it was a brilliant reply. He was just as up for the fun as I was.

The results show came very quickly and I felt it was my time to go. Before I even knew what was happening, James and Ella were standing in the bottom two. I thought I was dreaming. This wasn't right, both of these people should be in the final, they're both potential winners. It was my brother versus my little sister. I ran to the side of the stage to tell them that I wanted to leave, it wasn't fair, both of them deserved to stay. I'd had my fun, this was the time to bow out gracefully and leave the real contenders to do their thing. I tried to get up on the stage but I was being held back by floor managers and researchers. 'It's a public vote! You can't do anything about it legally!' I wasn't listening, I just wanted them both to stay. I was in a state. They explained that even if I did walk away, one of those two would still have to go as it's a public vote and legally people have paid money, so it wouldn't change anything. I was absolutely devastated. Ella was eliminated and I've never been in a studio even to this day where you could hear a pin drop as you could then. Everyone was upset. I held Ella like a baby for about ten minutes. She was fine. I wasn't. My family and her family became really close, so it was a loss for both sides.

Week eight and it was the quarter-finals. How the fuck have I made it this far? I never intended in my wildest dreams to last through two months of live shows. I had even got to the stage where I had to sing two songs. It was Abba week. The show took me and my mum to see *Abba the Musical*, another dream come true, and I got some lovely feedback from the cast and crew. Surely by this point my time was up on the show. I just wanted to leave with dignity. I performed on the Saturday night and did what I could. Come Sunday I knew it was time. As I was standing behind the famous doors with James, Jahméne and Nicole, there was something I had to do. I put my hand in my back left pocket and pulled out my lucky stone. I looked at Nicole and she looked at me. I told her that I had had the best experience and I was so grateful she was there for me every step of the way. I gave her the stone and asked her to hold on to it for me. She looked at me, upset. I then said, 'But don't fucking get too comfortable, I want it back afterwards – it's my lucky fucking stone.' She burst into a fit of laughter and we walked through the doors.

Bottom two with Union J. I loved the boys to bits and always knew they'd be a great band. I wanted to leave with my head held high and sang 'Wires' by Athlete. Gary said it was my best performance of the series and the others agreed. It was my time to bow out gracefully and move on to the next chapter of my crazy journey. Despite the ups and the downs, the show was great to me. I played the show as much as the show played me. It's a machine, no one is bigger than the format. I had a job to do. It wasn't to win the thing, my job was to be the one everyone spoke about and give them a full-on show every Saturday night, and do you know what? I think I did my job well.

'This is Big Brother, would Frankie and Rylan please come to the diary room'

Big Brother 2013

13

After three hours' sleep it was time to say goodbye to the apartment and get back to reality. I felt like, in the weirdest possible way, that I had just been born. I was going to have to learn how to walk, talk, breathe . . . everything. It was like day one all over again. I was no longer in the show that had become my life. I felt distant from reality. After saying a teary goodbye to Alanda, I was whisked off to the ITV studios to appear on *Daybreak* and *This Morning*. I felt like shit on three hours' sleep, still the same hair from the night before. There was so much gel in it, it wouldn't even move when wet, and I literally got dressed in the dark – the lightbulb went out in the bedroom!

It was time for *Daybreak* and Lorraine Kelly's show.

She is one of those people who is always friendly and supportive rather than judgemental, unlike some other journalistic presenters. I was joined by Dan Wootton, showbiz journalist, who only a year before had slagged me off when I was on *Signed by Katie Price,* calling me 'ropey-looking'. This time he changed his tune and wished me luck on my journey.

Next up, time to go on *This Morning.* I was really nervous about going on, but Phil and Holly were brilliant and all I remember is that we just laughed and laughed. The worst thing happened though. I laughed and laughed SO much that my lip burst open and my collagen filler started to dribble out. I'd had a bit too much filler put in the week before. The fucking horror. Live TV and half my lip was spread across the floor. SOMEHOW it wasn't as awful as it could have been and we continued to laugh at the situation. I joked and said that I'd hit my lip on a wall before quickly telling the truth. I remember going into cosmetic-counter mode and piping up like I was Jackie Stallone: 'I have my lips filled, although you could have a lip filler bar put into your top lip, although mind, you might go off when going through an airport.' Someone shut me the fuck up. It was funny and I managed to

209

get through both interviews relatively unscathed . . . can't say the same for my lip. Throughout the rest of the day I had interviews with various press outlets. That evening I returned home to my mum's. It felt weird being back in my own bedroom after so long. I think for the first time in months, I fell straight a sleep.

One of the first discussions I had with my management at the time was about who my tour manager would be. They were keen to place me with this nice bloke, who seemed friendly, but I had other ideas. 'I know who I want to be my tour manager,' I said boldly. 'His name is Ben and here's his number.' My management told me that I couldn't use anyone outside their company as it takes a long while for clients and tour managers to build trust and the people they already had lined up they knew they could trust. I put my foot down. 'I made a promise and I want Ben.' And Veruca Salt got her way.

Ben laughed the second he turned up and said, 'Fuck me. How's your luck – you really did come through, didn't ya?' I knew instantly he would become one of my best friends, and more to the point I was over the moon he'd be there every step of the way with me. Later that week we did our first gig since the show, in Swindon, and then one of the best gigs you get to do when you leave the show, G-A-Y. My old fucking hangout, years and years of seeing people performing on that stage, and the time had finally come for me to get up and have a go. Earlier that evening, Ronan Keating had asked me to duet with him at his annual Emeralds & Ivy charity ball round the corner. It was such an honour to perform with him then go on to G-A-Y – and to make it even better they had booked Lucy Spraggan to come and perform before me, bringing the two naughty kids back together after what seemed like years apart. It was so special, not only because of the venue, but because Lucy was with me and all the paparazzi shit was behind us.

Daybreak had asked me to be their guest entertainment presenter for the following week. I'd only been out of *The X Factor* for one week and I already had my first presenting gig on ITV – not bad, eh? It went well with Lorraine and Aled. They were amazing to work with. They both pushed me to go into presenting as they said I had a natural ability for it. Lorraine especially has always been very pro-Rylan and I want to publicly thank her for always being so kind, especially from the very beginning.

Running up to Christmas and New Year I hardly had an hour off. I was performing all over the country every night, sometimes three cities a night. It was fucking exhausting. My old mates James, Katy and the girls would come to gigs for the ride and a night out, and we'd all make sure we had a great time. I also got very close to Aaron, the dancer from *The X Factor* who'd rescued me from dangling wires. Out of everyone he probably understood the most what I had gone through as he was there with me through it all. A few weeks leaving the show I finally had the conversation with management about *Celebrity Big Brother.* As I'd suspected, they were not happy. They thought that it would be the wrong move for me and if I wanted to be taken seriously in this industry then I shouldn't go near it. I was gutted. I really wanted to do it. I didn't want to start rowing with my management, but I knew what I wanted and it felt right to me. I wasn't going to take this lying down. I pleaded with them to let me do it, but in fact what I didn't know was that my *X Factor* contracts prohibited me from doing any other type of reality show for the next three months anyway. Now I was fucking gutted, I couldn't believe it. 1: Legally I couldn't do it, and 2: My management aren't exactly going to fight my corner if they don't want me to do it in the first place. Then something great happened. Two weeks before Christmas I got the call that I now know pretty much changed my life. Without naming names, someone VERY high up at Channel 5 called someone VERY high up at Syco. They had words, and after a bit of to-ing and fro-ing, I was finally allowed to do *Big Brother*. I couldn't believe it. It was finally happening, six years after I should have walked through those famous doors. In a few weeks' time I'd be doing it for real, on the *celebrity version*! WHAT IS MY FUCKING LIFE?

I had a few free days at Christmas and spent it at home with my family. Myself and my mum went to my brother's house for Christmas dinner. It was lovely spending time with Jamie, Jayne, Harvey and Olivia, and my mum, all of us under one roof. My nan was at my Auntie Sue's so I knew she was being spoilt as well. For the past few months I'd hardly seen them. Just being Ross for the day was exactly what I needed, a break from my new crazy reality.

In the week running up to New Year I was back out on the road again with Ben. I had grown so close to him, to the point where he knew everything about me, and I knew everything about him: inside leg measurement, girth, the lot . . . I knew I could trust him and classed him as one of my best friends. On New Year's Eve I was performing in a club in Cork, Ireland. Aaron had flown over to see me as this was my last performance before going into *Celebrity Big Brother*. That evening Aaron gave me a bracelet to wish me luck in the house. I promised him I'd wear it every eviction night (which I did). I knew that was the last time I'd be on stage without anyone knowing who I *really* was. People just knew me as Rylan from *The X Factor*, no one really knew the real me behind it all. That's what I had to show in *Celebrity Big Brother* – the real side to me, not the stage side.

Back in London I spent New Year's Eve indoors at home with my mum. Not very rockstar at all, but the following day I was to be taken into hiding for the *second* time in my life. We watched the fireworks on the telly at midnight and were in bed by one. I didn't sleep that night. Not one bit. After all these years my time was coming. I was going into *Big Brother*. I spent a long time thinking back to the time I went to the old house in Bow with my friend Ashleigh, throwing clothes pegs over the garden wall. And the time I was in hiding in the Lake District when I was eighteen, naively thinking my life was about to change. All those years of waiting and wanting it was actually happening, the contract was signed and it was *really happening.*

I got up at 9 a.m. The car was booked to collect me at midday. My mum was already up as she always was and asked me if I wanted a bacon sandwich. It all seemed very normal. My stomach was turning and I couldn't eat a thing. I remember her saying, 'You've got to eat something or you'll be fucking ill.' Standard Linda phrase. We both sat there making sure I had everything packed. 'Have you got enough pants? What about socks? Do you want me to put a roll in there for later?' she kept asking, worriedly, as if I was about to go to a North Korean war camp. '*No, Mum!* I'm all right,' I kept saying on repeat. The car turned up bang on midday. I said my quick goodbye to my mum and jumped in. The driver had no idea who I was or what I was going to do. He got lost on the way to the hotel we were all being kept in. He must have had a right old fright when we eventually turned up and I was bundled out of the car by production members with a black blanket thrown over my head. It was like I was being abducted.

I was taken into a hotel room where I met Ros. She gave me a massive cuddle and was just as excited as I was that I was finally there. She introduced me to a girl called Kellie, who was going to be my chaperone for the next two days until I entered the house. She cracked me right up. 'Hello, tinker. We're gonna have a wicked time. I looked after Natalie Cassidy last time, so you've got a good 'un here.' She made me die. I knew I'd get on with her instantly.

For the next forty-eight hours I was to be locked in this hotel room, not allowed to leave unless it was for filming purposes or photoshoots for the series. Couldn't be that bad, could it? My phone was confiscated again. Here we go. My suitcase was opened and all of my clothes were being checked, debranded and written down. Then it happened. The door opened and a guy brought in my brand-new *Celebrity Big Brother* suitcases. My heart went. This has happened to me before . . . Flashback to that same moment six years ago. I wasn't going to make that same mistake again. They were bright pink and very on-trend, if I do say so myself. I just played it cool. After hours of my clothes being assessed and put into the shiny new cases, I started to feel the cabin fever. I needed to get out of the room, but I wasn't allowed. Kellie wasn't allowed to let me out of the room. Fuck this, I thought. I opened the door and said, 'You coming with me?'

She looked at me, slightly scared as to what might happen. 'Bollocks, let's do it,' she said. (Told you I'd get on well with her.)

We crept down the fire escape, hoping not to be seen by anyone, slid out of an exit door, and made our way through the service entrance to . . . THE BINS. Yes, the fucking bins. My best MI5-type escape in years and I've ended up at the bins. We stayed there for about forty minutes. We had a lovely time. Who knew you could have so much fun round the back of the bins, eh? Over the next two days I had my housemate pictures done, some *Big Brother's Bit on the Side* fun packs to complete, along with some psych question packs to fill out. I was kept well occupied. The night before I entered the house, Jamie, my hairdresser, came to the room to cut my hair. He wished me luck and off he went. The producers also let me have a spray tanner come and spray me. By this point I had a good idea who was going into the house with me as it was being heavily covered in the press. I asked Kellie to go and knock on Claire from Steps' door and ask if she wanted a spray tan on me as a little 'I fuck-ing love you and can't wait to meet you'-type gesture. Kellie, being the absolute ledge that she is, went and asked. She came back in the room with her smile and said, 'Claire from Steps don't do spray tans, but she said thank you for the offer and she can't wait to meet you tomorrow.' LIFE FUCKING MADE.

I slept surprisingly well that night. Seven a.m., bright and early, the tinker herself, Kellie, wakes me up singing 'The Final Countdown', genuinely. She told me it was time to go to the studios and go into the holding room on site. IT WAS FINALLY HERE. I put on my best onesie and was taken down the fire escape to where the car was parked. I was given a rubber mask to wear and all the windows of the car had black tape across them. I could see out of the windscreen we were making our way down Borehamwood High Street. 'On the left is where they film *EastEnders* with old Nat Cass,' Kellie said. I felt like I was in Hollywood, not Borehamwood. Then I see the entrance to Elstree Studios, the home of *Big Brother*. 'We're here!' she said with a beaming smile on her face.

My heart started racing and I thought I was having a

fucking heart attack. All I kept thinking is, It's finally happening, after all these years it's finally happening. I started to really work myself up and just couldn't control it. I was taken to a little white room where I would spend the rest of the day. Now, I understand why they put you in rooms like that before you go in. It's to get you used to being under lock and key, but at the time I was getting really frustrated. In my room was a small window that opened about half a centimetre. Every time I'd hear a car arrive I'd pop my eyeball as far out as I could to catch a glimpse of who it could be. After an hour of confinement I heard a car door. I popped my eyelash round and see her. CLAIRE FROM FUCKING STEPS LOOKING LIKE CRUELLA DE VIL IN A BLACK ONESIE AND RUBBER MASK. She could have been covered in human shit and I would have *still* been star-struck. My first thought was, Will she like me? My second thought was, Think of all the Steps songs we'll be able to sing and dance to together in the house!!! My third thought was, She's gonna fucking hate me singing Steps songs all the time, ain't she? Fuck it, I'll do it anyway.

I was in that room for fourteen hours all in all. Popped my head out a few times and see Tricia Penrose aka

Gina from *Heartbeat* having a sly cigarette in a lovely sparkly gown. 'ALL RIGHT, GINA!' I shouted from the window.

''ELLO, DARLIN! CAN'T WAIT TO GIVE YA A CUDDLE!' she replied, before a nervous member of production pushed her back into the hallway. She seemed decent.

I knew Toadfish from *Neighbours* was next door because I could hear him talking to someone in his strong Australian accent. It was all getting increasingly real to me. A bit too real. At 8 p.m. I was ready and raring to go, although for the first time my *Big Brother* experience really hit me. The Fear set in. What if I fuck it up? What if everyone hates me? AND the worst one . . . WHAT IF I'M EVICTED FIRST?! THE FUCKING SHAME OF IT ALL!!! I was having a proper panic. Kellie tried to calm me down and she did a good job, but as I kept reminding her, even Nat Cass went second or third. I ain't as well liked as Sonia and her trumpet, now am I?!

The time was now. It was time to legitimately become a housemate. I was put into a car for a twenty-second ride up to the house. As I opened the door I could hear the crowds roar. I was taken on to the orbit stage and placed behind the mechanical eye to the catwalk. Ros was standing there and asked if I was all right.

I just stood there, silent . . .

'Rylan?'

'RYLAN!?'

'Are you OK?'

I wasn't. I felt completely numb. I could hear my entrance video playing on the big screen. People were cheering but then I heard a couple of them boo. And for the first time I had the worst thought I could have had.

'I can't do it, Ros, I don't want to do it.'

After all these years, I didn't want to do it. I couldn't put my family through all that again.

Then the eye opened to the catwalk.

I'd planned this walk my *entire* life – smile, pose, lap it up. But all I could think was, GET ME INSIDE THAT FUCKING HOUSE PRONTO, I HATE IT.

Watching it back now, I don't remember doing it. It was nothing like the walk I'd practised as a twelve-year-old little ginger kid. I grabbed Brian Dowling's hand for dear life. All of a sudden Frankie Dettori was standing next to me. 'What's going on? This ain't right, this ain't right!'

I kept shrieking. We were the first two housemates and were to be set a mission. HARK AT ME ON *CELEBRITY BIG BROTHER* WITH A MISSION before we'd even entered the house! We had some very cold, hard decisions to make. We then made the walk up the stairs and through the famous doors. As I heard the doors shut behind me that was it. I knew I had finally done it. It was like entering my dream. The mirrors in the walls, the big staircase, the little eyes that light up above all the doors that signal if they're locked or unlocked. Frankie seemed really casual and not fazed by any of it. Then it happened . . .

'THIS IS BIG BROTHER. WOULD FRANKIE AND RYLAN PLEASE COME TO THE DIARY ROOM . . .'

Oh my fucking Big Brother God. I just got called to the diary room by Big Brother. You could see the excitement on my face. Frankie, still as casual as a cucumber, even though I'm repeatedly saying to him, 'The diary room, Frank, the diary room. We're going to the diary room, Frank!'

I sat down on the actual diary room chair, which was a block of ice with a fur throw. It was the most unreal feeling. Big Brother instructed us that we would have to choose which housemates would be sent to the dirty basement, and which housemates would join us in the main house. We would see their entrance videos and decide by a series of questions Big Brother asked us who would go down, and who would come up. We chose to send Tricia Penrose, Gillian Taylforth (Kathy Beale to me), Claire from Steps and Lacey Banghard into the main house and Paula Hamilton, Ryan Moloney (Toadfish), 'Razor' Ruddock and Sam Robertson to the basement. They all took it in jest as they knew it was a game.

Finally Big Brother faced us with our final dilemma. The next two housemates were Heidi and Spencer from America. They were famous for being the villains on American reality TV, but I always wondered if this was an act on their part. I guess I would find out soon enough. The dilemma was whether we send both of them to the basement, or myself and Frankie go down to the basement. Now, I'd like to think I'm a gentleman . . . Until I watched their entrance video saying they had seen the rumoured line-up and that we all looked like weirdos. ALL THE BEST, BABE. YOU'RE BOTH GOING DOWN.

Selfish or not selfish, I still think we made the right

choice. We were then free to join the girls in the main house. I finally got to give Tricia her cuddle and meet Claire from Steps. They were all so lovely. We were let into the garden and an area had been sectioned off like a prison. The basement housemates finally emerged to introduce themselves and they were all really sweet and harboured no hard feelings . . . Apart from two of them, Heidi and Spencer. They were 'too tired' to come and say hello. I found it a bit weird but I didn't let it bother me. I had a feeling, though, that they weren't going to be easy.

Over the course of the following few days I connected with everyone. I formed a close bond with Frankie, Claire, Razor and Gillian. They were my core group. Everyone had moved into the main house and the basement task was over. Heidi and Spencer proved to be quite difficult and were evidently game players. I'm not going to bore you with the ins and outs of every task during my time on *Celebrity Big Brother*, but I came to blows with them on several occasions. They just weren't playing nice. They were so out for themselves and didn't take part in most things we were meant to do as a team. I didn't know if it was a game they were playing or if they both just were vile, nasty bastards. I rowed with them both so much during my time in there I was worried how I was coming across to the public. For all I knew the public loved them and hated me for challenging their behaviour. You genuinely know nothing. It's like a world within a world. But to me *Celebrity Big Brother* was like therapy. At the time, everyone on the outside wanted a piece of me, a picture, an interview, a scandal. Being in that house allowed me to regroup a bit. If I hadn't have gone in I genuinely don't think I'd be where I am today. For most people I'd heard it messes with their heads. For me it sorted mine out.

Times did get hard in there. I worried about my mum constantly and I thought of her more than ever. Of course I knew that if anything was wrong my family would tell Big Brother and I'd be told, but she was always on my mind. I'd already witnessed how much my nan had deteriorated. I hoped that she would be watching, understanding everything that was going on, but deep down I think she was watching thinking that I was just at home and she was there too, which gave me a lot of comfort.

One evening I was having a pretty normal conversation with Frankie. He hadn't watched *The X Factor* so knew almost nothing about me. All he knew was that I was a sort of hate figure and that generally people didn't like me. Which for the most part I already knew, but for some reason his comments upset me. I started worrying what people were thinking of me now that I was in the house. I went and sat in the toilet and cried like a girl. I was so worried that my mum was out there defending me, and I was convinced that my brother and all of my family were having to stick up for me like they had during *The X Factor.* Frankie thought he had said something wrong, but he hadn't. It meant a lot to me that he and most of the other housemates assured me that I was doing well and hadn't let myself down.

I had the best three and a half weeks in there. I cried, I laughed, I cried again, and it all culminated in the ultimate final. Razor, Claire, Toadfish, Heidi and Spencer, and me. We all sat around on the sofas, knowing it was our last few hours together in the house. Everyone was so excited to get out and see their friends and family. I was as well, although I was upset that it was all coming to an end. I'd waited my whole life to do this show. I was going to miss it in there. Fifth place was announced and Razor was evicted. Fourth place was announced and Claire from Steps was evicted. I was gutted because I was so close to the pair of them. If Razor had become like a father figure then Claire was like my big sister. Third place was announced and Toadfish was evicted. I couldn't believe it. It was me versus Heidi and Spencer. Good vs bad. The final showdown. Over the past twenty-three days I had had *the* most turbulent time with those two. They'd played a good game and gave a great show but it would have killed me to come second to them. Anyone else I could have dealt with, but not them.

Watching *Big Brother* growing up, whenever the final two were shown, there they would be, side by side, holding hands and wishing each other luck, but it wasn't like that this time. They sat on the sofa across from where I was sitting. They could have been sat all the way back in America we were so separate. '*Celebrity Big Brother* house, this is Brian. Heidi and Spencer, Rylan, your time has come,' Brian's voice echoed. I could hear the crowds outside chanting 'RYLAN!' but it didn't mean anything to me. I kept thinking back to Nat Cass and how she was evicted early and everyone was shocked. I really thought for that moment Heidi and Spencer had done it. They had upset everyone in that house and they were going to walk out winners. To them it was just another pay cheque, but to me it was years of wanting. 'For the last seven days the great British public have been voting for their winner. I can now reveal the celebrity housemate with the most votes and the winner of *Celebrity Big Brother* is . . .' My heart stopped. The crowds cheers seemed to disappear and I completely shut off. The ten or so seconds seemed like hours. I just realised that it didn't matter what happened, I'd done what I came to do. I could hear the crowds chanting my name and I'd made it to the final – I must've done something right. Then he announced it.

'RYLAN!'

I COULDN'T FUCKING BELIEVE IT. I'VE ONLY GONE AND FUCKING WON IT! I felt like collapsing. Heidi and Spencer's game faces dropped and they came and congratulated me. It was like they'd been playing characters for the last three weeks and now the real them showed. They both seemed genuinely happy for me. They made their way up the stairs and left. I was alone in the *Big Brother* house. I had done it. I had finally done it. My first thought was that my mum would be proud, as would all of my family. It meant so much. For the five minutes I was left alone in the house, Big Brother spoke to me. 'Hello, Rylan. Congratulations, you've been a great housemate. Well done.' It was the first time during my whole stay that Big Brother actually sounded like a person with real emotions and seemed happy for me. I said out loud, 'This has been brilliant, so thank you, everyone.' I meant it from the bottom of my heart.

I walked up the famous stairs, trying to take in every last ounce of the house, as I knew I'd never be back. I turned to take one last look and blew a kiss to the house. I turned around and the doors opened. I took the winner's walk down the stairs. As I reached the catwalk I remembered back to launch night. How I'd felt back then. Worried I'd fuck it up. Worried people wouldn't understand or get me. And twenty-three days later I was standing in the same spot, the winner, with everyone chanting my name and the rest of the housemates all looking so pleased for me. I was so lucky I couldn't believe it. I went on to *Big Brother's Bit on the Side* straight after with Emma Willis and everything seemed like a blur. All my trusted friends, James, Katy and Aaron, were there.

That evening I had to do my press interviews straight away as the following day I was going on the *X Factor* arena tour. I finished up at around 4 a.m. I was driven back to my mum's house by Ben. It was such a relief to see him. I felt a bit lost without him. The team was back together.

I arrived at my mum's at 5 a.m. She gave me the biggest cuddle and said how proud of me she was. I had an hour's sleep, swapped my *Big Brother* cases for my tour cases and got back into the car with Ben. We drove three and a half hours to Manchester for the start of the tour.

I was knackered, but I wasn't going to miss opening night for the world.

'I'd gone from bubble to bubble to bubble, and finally the bubble was about to burst'

Rylan Ross Clark 2013

14

Ten a.m. Manchester Arena. Twelve hours ago I'd been announced as the winner of *Celebrity Big Brother*. I'd seen my mum for what seemed like ten minutes and I was already back working. I arrived with Ben and was taken to my dressing room. The choreographer Beth came in and gave me a hug. I felt truly out of it. I'd hardly had any sleep and could have collapsed there and then, but there's no rest for the wicked. I was taken into an empty arena and put on the stage. Because I'd been in isolation I had a lot to catch up on. The dancers were ready and we were all excited to be there – most of them were from the live shows anyway, so it was nice to see some familiar faces. A few hours later the rest of the finalists arrived. James, Jahméne, Ella, Christopher, the

Having the teeth put in.

Look at her… just love her!

Me and Ben – he fucking loves it!

Me and Debbie x.

The last picture taken of me,
Mummy and Nanny.

My gorgeous Nanny Rose in the home,
she had a good laugh about the teeth.

Me and Spraggan two years on.

Me and my Helen – "2 Girls!"

The tele mum and dad.

One of my *Big Brother* press shots.

Me and gorgeous Emma.

Rylan McDonald, Happy Meals for the team at BB.

Myself, Grayson and the Earl of Essex.

The night we got engaged… before the rats.

Mummy and Wendy.

We're engaged x

Me, Dan and my stepson, Cameron.

When the Neal boys became four …

The 'STEN' do.

Casual wedding foliage shot.

Me and my cousin Kimberley the night before I got married.

We did it!

Mummy, Jamie, me, Dan, Wendy and Steve.

The bridesmaids!

Union J and District 3 boys all ran up to me and congratulated me. I'd missed them. Before we even had time to catch up we were in hair and make-up and getting ready for the opening night.

I felt really strange. It didn't feel right being able to walk outside or go into any room I wanted without Big Brother locking the door.

During the tour, it was down to me to open the show so I was always first on. I made my way up to the stage and behind the gigantic doors where the dancers were waiting. They were all ready and raring to go. I was excited but felt like I was having a bit of an out-of-body experience. I didn't feel like I was actually there. I could hear the crowds cheering and screaming and it all seemed surreal. I looked at one of my dancers and asked her if it was all going to be all right. She simply smiled and said, 'You're gonna smash it.'

My name was announced and the doors started to open. The screams were so loud I could even feel the crowd's breath on my face. As I opened my mouth to sing my opening line, I froze. Staring at me were 11,000 faces in a huge arena. I was used to seeing the same ten faces for the last three weeks. I just froze and started to cry.

233

It was too much. I wasn't ready for it. The crowd could see I was upset and screamed and chanted even more. The sound crew could see I was in a state and restarted my song. It was so overwhelming, within the space of twenty-four hours to go from locked up in the *Big Brother* house to performing in front of 11,000 people literally overnight. Add to that the fact of only an hour's sleep and you can start to understand how emotional I was. I sang the first lines and the show went on.

I managed to get through the whole show and went straight to the hotel we were all staying in. I went to bed at 11 p.m. and slept all the way through to 11 a.m. The following night, after the show, all the crew threw me a surprise 'Congratulations, you won *Big Brother*' party at the Living Room in Manchester, a super-nice club. I got so pissed I had to be carried out of there by the security team. I really didn't care though; if anything, I fucking needed it. I felt like a complete fish out of water. I didn't even know my own name.

The following day I was allowed to miss the tour bus to the next city so I could properly catch up on my sleep. The crew had arranged for Ben to come and pick me up later that evening to drive me to our next destination as we had a rest day. I woke up around midday disorientated and straight away called Ella. She told me that they had all already left and would see me later that evening. I called Ben and he told me he would be with me at around 5 p.m. For the first time in as long as I could remember, I was alone. No one around me. No friends, no security, no Big Brother, nothing.

I started to panic. I can only describe how I felt like a dream I once had. You know that dream where you're in bed and you're sleeping against a wall; you wake up and turn over to find that there is another wall right next to you and you're boxed in and can't escape. That's how I felt. I wanted to have a cigarette but was too frightened to venture downstairs on my own. I was going to have one in the room but was scared someone who worked in the hotel would knock on the door. I couldn't think of anything worse than facing anyone I didn't know alone. I started having a panic attack.

I called Ben, who told me he had already left so would be with me earlier than planned. I was crying. What the fuck is happening to me? I'm a grown man. I couldn't understand what was going on in my head and what was making me so nervous of everything. I didn't move for the next four hours. I just sat there in silence until Ben finally arrived and I threw my arms around him for dear life. I was a wreck. I couldn't stand to be alone. For the past however many months, I'd never been fully alone anywhere at any time. I quickly realised this was a problem but didn't know how to solve it. I asked Ben if he would stay with me for the whole of the tour and he agreed. Logistically it was a nightmare, but until I felt safe and in that routine I couldn't not be with him. I paid for his hotel rooms and petrol out of my own pocket. Even though I had the tour crew, I hadn't rehearsed with them or met them so they weren't familiar to me. Ben stayed for the first two weeks of the tour until I really settled in. I started feeling a lot more comfortable, and having the other *X Factor* finalists around me made it feel a lot more like home.

Speaking of home, the tour reached the O2. I grew up literally minutes away, over the water in Stepney, so for me this was the place where I've always wanted to perform. We turned up at the venue via the artists' entrance. The last time I'd been there was for my first *X Factor* audition. It really hit me hard walking the long corridors backstage, seeing the icons who had performed in the very same venue. Now people were coming and paying money to see me and my friends perform. It was made extra special by the fact that all of my family and friends were coming, including my mum. Some of my *Big Bro* housemates came along as well to support me.

For me it was the best show to date. I could see my family and friends in the audience, especially my best friend James, who was crying every five minutes because he couldn't actually believe I'd done it. We all had drinks afterwards and laughed into the early hours. Then we left and carried on with the rest of the tour. But the fear of the outside world hadn't left me. I physically couldn't go *anywhere* on my own. It wasn't the fact that I was frightened something bad would happen, it was more the fear of the unknown. People would look at me everywhere I went. I'm six feet four and quite recognisable; I couldn't exactly 'blend in'. It seemed like everyone wanted a piece of me. The fear would always hit me the hardest whenever someone noticed me and started walking towards me. Are they going to want a photo? An autograph? Are they going to punch me directly in the face? All of these scenarios would play out in my head over the five seconds I had to actually think about it.

Most of the time people were friendly, but on the odd occasion people weren't so nice. People would shout things like 'gay' 'queer cunt', etc. Naturally it would upset me. I think mainly because of the fact that I hadn't had the time to appreciate what had happened to me. I'd not treated myself to anything. Towards the end of the tour I started to become a bit of a recluse. I wouldn't want to go out and party like I used to. I wouldn't go *anywhere* without the security team, and I'd find myself starting to make excuses for not attending events or friends' or family parties. I didn't know what was going on in my head. I lost all elements of free will, not because it had been taken away from me, but because I had chosen subconsciously to remove it from my life for fear of the unknown. In the back of my mind I knew that once the tour was over, that was it. I didn't know what the future would hold for me. I'd gone from *The X Factor* to *Celebrity Big Brother* on to a whirlwind tour of Britain. I'd gone from bubble to bubble to bubble, and finally the bubble was about to burst.

'I can see what you've done to get here, and I applaud you.'

Grayson Perry 2013

15

I remember receiving a call from my management informing me that Grayson Perry had been in touch and wanted to work with me. I instantly thought I had heard wrong and answered, 'Why does Lady Penelope want to work with me? She's a cartoon character, ain't she?' I soon realised that it was in fact the real-life artist of our generation, Grayson Perry himself. The idea was that he was going to follow a few people and learn about their lives for a Channel 4 documentary called *Grayson Perry: Who Are You?* Each person he spoke to had been through something in their life – for example, someone who'd had a sex change, someone who'd converted religions – and I would be the one who'd found fame overnight. He wanted to come and meet me and get to know me, film with me for a bit and, ultimately, make a piece of art that would be on show in the National Portrait Gallery in London. I couldn't believe what I was hearing. Rylan from *The X Factor* will be on show in the National Portrait Gallery??? That's fucking bizarre.

When Grayson came to meet me at my mum's house, I expected him to be dressed as his alter ego 'Claire', but he turned up looking like himself in a pair of trousers and T-shirt. He was lovely. A really nice gentleman who seemed genuinely interested in what I had to say. I knew we would get on the second he turned to me and said, 'I can see who you really are, and I know exactly what you've done to get here, and I applaud you.' This was the moment that I realised that someone as clever, interesting and important as he was could see me for who I *really* was, not who the public thought I was. As he began to interview me, I found myself completely opening up to him. He then asked to sketch me sitting on my diary room chair, which I had robbed after I won *Celebrity Big Brother*. I remember sitting and being drawn by him and realising how lucky I was that this was all happening. The man is an absolute genius. The moment was quickly ruined by my mum Linda shouting from the kitchen, 'GRAYSON, YOU COULDN'T MAKE ME ONE OF YOUR URNS FOR THE TOP OF MY STAIRS, COULD YA?!' Trust Linda to lower the tone! Grayson laughed and politely agreed, with no genuine intention of doing it – I doubt Linda has a few hundred thousand to spare . . .

We then had the pleasure of going back to my childhood home in Stepney, East London. Grayson wanted to understand my upbringing and where I came from. We arrived at Stepney Green Road and the house where I spent my first twelve years, and a lovely lady called Kim agreed to let us in and look around. The house felt so much smaller than I remembered it, perhaps because I had grown another five feet since I was last there, but still . . . Kim asked if my real name was Ross. I answered simply, 'Yes.' She led me over to the cupboard under the stairs and told me to look inside. Amongst all the usual stuff you would find in a cupboard under the stairs, there, in rainbow-coloured crayon, scrawled over the back wall were the words 'ROSS SPICE GIRLS 97'. It choked me up. In front of me was a snapshot of my childhood that I didn't even remember existed. 'For some reason I didn't paint over it; it seemed wrong to cover it up,' Kim explained. It was such a special moment to be in the house I grew up in, knowing I had definitely left my mark – along with Geri, Emma, Mel B, Mel C and Victoria . . .

Grayson also followed me during the early days of hosting *Bit on the Side*. He wanted to meet Rylan as well as Ross. Then, after a week or two, off he went into the sunset to make the rest of his TV series and, more importantly, start working on the art for his *Who Are You?* exhibition at the National Portrait Gallery in London.

After a year had passed, it was finally time to see the piece of art he had made based on me. I arrived in London's Trafalgar Square around 6.30 a.m., as we needed to film the reactions of the subjects before the gallery was opened to the public. I was taken into a beautiful room, surrounded by art from hundreds of years ago. There Grayson stood, looking at me. I had no idea about what he had made – whether it was a drawing, a pot, a scarf – no idea at all. 'Here it is,' he said sheepishly, hoping I would like it. There I was, little old Ross from Stepney Green, immortalised in enamel and plaster of Paris as a miniature entitled 'The Earl of Essex'. I couldn't believe it. I was completely overwhelmed. The description was as follows:

> Rylan has become famous in a very short period of time. In some ways celebrities are like the aristocracy of our times and I have portrayed him on a miniature in the style of the Elizabethan court. Rylan's striking looks brought to mind a dandyish nobleman as portrayed by Nicholas Hilliard. The fame Rylan pursues comes at a cost in that it unbalances relationships with strangers and friends alike. The miniature implies a lost intimacy and also echoes the smartphone-screen natural home of the 21st century celebrity portrait.

Grayson looked at me and thanked me for being part of his experience, and I thanked him in return. He reminded me that he had asked for a lock of my hair back when he sketched me originally and told me that my hair was encased inside the miniature and that I will be part of that piece of art for ever. It made it all that more personal, something that not many people would know. Grayson, I can't thank you enough for choosing to work with me. You are a visionary of amazement. The series got great reviews and won a BAFTA . . . something I am proud to be part of.

'Them fucking teeth!"

Linda Clark 2013

16

On the final night of the *X Factor* tour I found out that my lovely Nanny Rose had suffered a small stroke. Over the course of the last few months the Alzheimer's had taken its toll, and something that once seemed ever so slightly funny and we could make a joke out of suddenly become much worse. I knew there was talk of her going into a home and I couldn't let that happen. None of us wanted that. I've got the best family and we're all there for each other – there's no way this could happen.

My nan was still living with my Auntie Sue at the time, because it was easier as she lived in a bungalow. I focused on the final night of the tour and tried to block it all out. The last performance went smoothly in Belfast and we all flew home the next day. When we arrived at Heathrow Airport it was time to say our final goodbyes. The *X Factor* journey was over. We were standing around the baggage carousel hugging, crying, and wishing it wasn't over. We were all very close, without a doubt, but deep down we had learned by now that in this industry nothing lasts for ever. We didn't know when we'd next see each other, or if in fact we'd see each other again at all. Ben picked me up at the airport and we made our way back to Essex. I arrived home to my mum's house. She made me a tea and I took my suitcases upstairs to my bedroom. I sat on my bed and broke down crying. It was all over. Apart from a few personal appearances in the diary there was nothing for me to really get excited about, no more bubbles for me to submerge myself in.

I was given a few days off to try and sort my head out. I'd noticed that I hadn't been my usual self for a while and could see that I wasn't comfortable being 'RYLAN'. I'd look on Twitter and Facebook and see comments by complete strangers slagging me off and calling me every name under the sun. What have I created? My name is Ross, I'm not this person people keep saying I am. Looking back now, the bad comments were few and far between and there were many other lovely ones. My stint on *Celebrity Big Brother* really had changed people's perceptions of me but I couldn't help being bothered by the small minority that were still out to kill off The *X Factor* character. I only had myself to blame – I'd created him, I was the one who'd played along week in week out, trying to make something of myself. I remember ringing Katie Price – she'd been through it for years. I needed to talk to someone who not only knew what I was going through, but someone who had conquered the shit. She told me to not give a flying fuck and carry on being me. She'd created Jordan, I'd created Rylan, DEAL WITH IT.

Over the next few weeks I did the odd job on television. An appearance on *Celebrity Juice*, a few items on *This Morning* talking about onesies and fake tan, and a few other panel shows. I needed something that was more full-time and would keep my mind occupied. SOMEONE must have been looking down on me because that's when the phone call came. The people at *Big Brother* had asked to meet me to discuss 'working together'. WHAT? Cue the catchphrase of the last year: IS THIS A FUCKING WIND-UP? Work with me on what?! It was all quite unclear what they had in mind, but nonetheless I was excited.

The meeting took place on a Tuesday in a private members' club in Notting Hill. I was introduced to a man called Nick Samwell-Smith. He was the head of Initial at Endemol, the company that makes *Big Brother*. He was very charming but also *very important*. He had that sort of air about him that was quite intimidating, but at the same time he was incredibly friendly. After a casual chat about my time in *Celebrity Big Brother* he said, 'So, we're having a bit of a change this year and we were wondering if you would be interested in hosting *Big Brother's Bit on the Side* . . . ?'

I looked at him.

He looked at me.

I looked at my manager.

She looked at me.

I looked at the waiter.

He ignored me in all honesty . . . But back to the chat . . .

What was I hearing? I'm not a presenter. Why the fuck does he think I'm capable of doing this? He went on to explain the idea. I was to be paired up with another presenter and we could present the show together. He had a few people in mind but initially wanted to see if it was something I'd want to do. I could have physically bitten his hand off and eaten it in front of him, but very calmly I said, 'That's something I'd love to do.' Thank you Mr Nick Samwell-Smith.

We shook hands on it and I made my way to Ben who was waiting outside. I casually slipped into the car and told him what I'd just been asked. He looked at me and his jaw dropped lower than the handbrake. He knew just as much as I did that this was exactly what I needed. Let's be honest, most *X Factor* contestants disappear off the face of the earth after the tour, and that's even if they were lucky enough to make the tour in the first place. Just as I thought my luck was inevitably running out, I was thrown a lifeline.

It wasn't a done deal just yet though. I had to go to the *Bit on the Side* studio and do a screen test, a little piece to camera with the girl they were hoping to pair me up with. A few weeks later I dolled myself up to the eyeballs and, whilst absolutely shitting myself, walked into the studio looking as cool as a cucumber. I was greeted by a very nice guy called Rich Smith – he was the executive producer, a really nice bloke who I instantly bonded with. He introduced me to AJ Ododu. She was absolutely stunning. I recognised her from a few things she had done previously and she was happy to chat about presenting work she had done before. It seemed she was just as nervous as I was – this was quite a big gig even for her, let alone for me. We got on well and I knew I'd be happy for her to be Ant to my Dec. The screen test was quite casual, asking us to talk about previous housemates, dream housemates, etc. I left feeling good about how it had gone and, more importantly, feeling like AJ was a decent girl – after all, she could have been a whole lot different, if you know what I mean. A week or so later we were told we'd both got the job. THANK ALL OF THE GODS, THANKS, JESUS, MOSES, THE DONKEY, EVERYONE, THANK YOU! I was fucking made up.

It was all meant to a bit of a secret until it was announced officially a few weeks later. I was told that Emma Willis would now be hosting the main show whilst also doing three days a week on *Bit on the Side,* and myself and AJ would be doing the other three days. One of the days would be my own show I'd host myself called *Rylan's Supersized Sunday.* It genuinely felt like I was dreaming – it was a permanent job, and my favourite show ever, *Big Brother.*

I had a month or so before *Big Brother* was back on TV, which is also around the same time I made probably the biggest, best/worst decision of my life. I decided to get my teeth done. I've always loved the look of veneers and since for ever always wanted to have them done myself. There was absolutely nothing wrong with my normal teeth but they were never 'perfect'. I've always wanted that perfect smile. I went for a consultation at a cosmetic dentist's surgery in Harley Street who were happy to do them for me. They asked if once they were finished they could use the pictures on their website for a bit of promotion, and me being me I was more than happy to oblige. By this point I was working every day, doing bits on *This Morning* and prepping for *Big Brother's Bit on the Side*. The actual 'putting the teeth in' and the work beforehand should not have taken any longer than a week or so. But given my schedule I'd have to go to the dentist's, have a little bit of work done, some temporary ones fitted, then return to work, and so on. This went on for around five weeks. I was so keen to make sure that my new teeth were all finished by the launch night of *Big Brother* that on one occasion I sat in the dentist's chair for around six hours, constantly being topped up with anaesthetic, to the point where the nursing assistant had to feed me liquid glucose because I was drifting in and out of consciousness. They needed to be finished. Finally, THE DAY BEFORE, I repeat, THE DAY BEFORE launch night, they were in. Now, I asked for white, and I also asked that most of my natural teeth weren't shaved away. I was told that because I wasn't having a lot shaved off my natural teeth, they might look a bit bigger to start off with until my mouth and face adjusted. None of the warnings bothered me in the slightest – I just wanted BIG WHITE PERFECT TEETH. I barely had time to look at them in the mirror before I had to go and get ready for my debut as a pre-senter on *Big Brother's Bit on the Side*. I was so fucking nervous. I couldn't even look on social media or speak to my family as it was so stressful. I hosted the first show alongside AJ and somehow managed to get through it. It was live, no retakes, pure, uncensored live TV. We didn't make too many errors and came off feeling rather proud. I was still finding it a bit hard to pronounce some words properly as I was still getting used to the veneers, and the anaesthetic was still having a little effect, but we did it nonetheless.

It wasn't until the car journey home that I finally managed to catch up with Twitter.

Rylan's teeth

Rylan

Teeth

Railings

Tombstones

. . . were all trending on Twitter . . .

I actually couldn't believe it. Even my mum's first reaction was "Them fucking teeth!" Looking back at some of the pictures people had screen-shot, my teeth looked like they were coming round the corner before I was. I was absolutely mortified I didn't realise that they would look *so white* against the shiny backdrop of the studio and my fake tan. They did, in all honesty, look completely ridiculous. In my defence they hadn't settled in properly and with hindsight I should have had them done *way* before I started at *Big Brother*, not twenty-four hours before. The following morning I woke up to find my picture splashed across most of the front pages of the tabloids. 'Rylan's teeth' was still trending on Twitter, and believe me they weren't admiring the view. I felt like I'd quickly slipped back into the role of national joke all over a set of fucking (if a little white) teeth. I was absolutely morti-fied. In real life they didn't actually look as bad as everyone was making out, but under the studio lights they REALLY showed up. I looked like I'd swallowed a torch. There was no way to tone them down without having them completely changed, but I just didn't have the time to do anything about them. The best thing about the opening two weeks on *Big Brother* was this: the fact that *everyone* was so busy talking about my teeth, no one really took notice of the fact that I wasn't a TV presenter, and the fact that I was actually quite shit at it in the beginning. The Brucie Bonus was I didn't get slated for my presenting skills, I got slated over my teeth, which in turn gave me time on the job to learn my craft as I went along, without anyone calling for me to be sacked. So the teeth gave me room to avoid too much scrutiny whilst I was still learning on the job. Touch.

It only took a few weeks before I started to settle in. I knew the show structure, learned to deal with someone talking in my ear at the same time as I'm talking, and, most of all, learned to have fun with it. So far my beloved *Big Brother* had changed my life and was giving me a career as a television presenter, but little did I know that the *Big Brother* fairy would wave it's magic wand again and change my personal life for ever.

On a separate note: the clinic never used the pictures of my teeth for promotion . . . shocker.

'On day forty-four Dan Neal was the sixth person to be evicted from the *Big Brother* house'

Rylan Ross Clark 2013

17

Work was going well. The teeth jokes stuck but by that point I really couldn't give a fuck. I was living the dream, presenting my dream show and genuinely loving life. Even so, my personal life was taking a hit. My Nanny Rose had become really bad with Alzheimer's and my family had no choice but to move her into a care facility. I was so against it – we all were – but there honestly wasn't anything else we could have done. Anyone who has been personally affected by Alzheimer's will know how hard it is to care for a loved one. One minute my nan would be making jokes, all laughter and smiles, the next minute she would become violent and lash out. This wasn't my nan – my nan was the best woman in the world. It got so bad that she didn't speak to my mum for three months for no reason whatsoever. It absolutely destroyed my mum and that's what worried me. The added stress of my nan's condition was making my mum worse. My aunties Sue and Pat and my mum found a care facility in Grays, Essex, which looked after people who suffered from Alzheimer's, and all agreed that it was the right place for my nan to be.

One Sunday, after presenting my Sunday show, I went there for the first time. I expected it to be full of loony people playing with their own piss, but I was gratefully wrong. It was a beautiful facility with a stunning garden and really nice staff. You hear the horror stories and always think the worst. I looked through the door and could see my nan sat very calmly speaking with another woman of a similar age. I walked in and gave my nan a cuddle; she seemed happy and couldn't wait to show me and my mum the garden. We sat on a bench and had a cup of tea. By this point my nan's speech wasn't what it used to be, but even with the Alzheimer's she couldn't resist a little joke. She took my sunglasses off, put them on, smiled the biggest smile, pointed at my teeth and had a little laugh. CHEEKY MARE! It made me feel amazing. In that moment she totally made me realise it doesn't matter what people say to me – as long as I can laugh at myself, who gives a fuck? We sat for an hour talking as well as we could, and my nan would try to explain who she liked in there and who she didn't. I won't repeat some of the things she said, but she did accuse someone of 'putting it about'. If she was right, I hope I'll still be able to do it at the age of the elderly woman she was speaking about. I left there with mixed feelings. I was sad, but at the end of the day my nan seemed very content and happy to be where she was, and that was good enough for me.

Back on *Big Brother*, eviction night soon arrived, and it was time for one housemate to face the chanting crowds on the outside. On day forty-four Dan Neal was the sixth person to be evicted from the *Big Brother* house. Dan was a policeman and had a thirteen-year-old son. Up until eviction he'd been a really good housemate, always up for a challenge, and could rumble one of Big Brother's secrets or lies easily. Unfortunately for him he didn't know he was up for eviction, as the one lie he didn't rumble was that in fact he wasn't safe and was up for the public vote. I felt sorry for him because it really came as a shock.

After doing his interview with Emma on the main show, it was time for me and AJ to give him a grilling on *Bit on the Side*. As he walked down the stairs I leaned in to give him a hug, as I do with all the housemates. THE BLOKE TOTALLY PIED ME OFF and rejected the hug and went for a handshake instead. MuggedOff.com. He seemed startled to be sat there, which was understandable seeing as he knew nothing about being nominated for eviction, but nevertheless he was a good interview. We invited him back to join my Sunday show and he seemed a lot more relaxed, friendlier and up for a laugh.

After the show had finished, I was having a cigarette, and he came out to have one too. We started chatting about the house and people left in there, especially Hazel, a girl who was still in the house who Dan had got close to. He told me that she had become a good mate and that he would miss her. We started talking about what Dan might do now he had left the house, seeing as there was no way he could go back to being a policeman. He asked me about managers and agents, etc., not knowing if he wanted/could do anything in my type of industry. I was more than happy to help him and gave him my number to drop me a text if he needed any advice or guidance when it came to stuff I knew about. I said goodbye and he left. There's no denying that Dan was very good-looking, and my initial impression that he was arrogant soon disappeared as he actually seemed like a decent chap. Dan had a boyfriend that he had been with for a few years, so there was no way I was going to say anything, but I sort of kind of liked him a bit. I'd learned the hard way years before, getting involved with people who had been with people or mates, etc. . . . Too messy. Forget about it.

Later that week Dan texted me asking some advice about a manager he had spoken to. As I didn't know what was going on I suggested a few to him personally. We met up one night to talk through people he had spoken to and agent stuff – nothing funny, purely business. I didn't understand why I was taking time out of my life to go and meet this bloke to help him with his career. Part of me obviously liked him, but I knew he was a no-go area. I dropped him home and went home myself. For a few weeks after I couldn't stop thinking about him. I didn't dare say anything to anyone at work because the unwritten rule is 'Don't get involved with housemates,' but it wasn't like that, he had a boyfriend. I'm not like that, and besides, I'm Rylan – he ain't gonna like me anyway. We continued texting strictly about work stuff over the following few weeks. It was strange because on the one hand the texts were all work-related, but on the other I was texting him because I actually quite liked him.

On 17 August it was Claire from Steps' birthday. I drove over to her house where she was having some close family and friends round to celebrate. Whilst I was there I received a phone call from Dan. He sounded excited. He told me that all was looking good on the work front and he had finally chosen someone to represent him. I was pleased for him. But then he told me that him and his boyfriend were no longer an item and had split up. I froze for a second, not knowing what to say. 'I just thought I'd let you know that,' he said into the silence. I quickly mumbled that I was sorry to hear it and said I'd speak to him later on. I got off the phone and immediately told Claire. She could see how much I clearly liked him and told me that if it's meant to be it's meant to be. I looked on his Twitter a few minutes later and realised that it was his birthday too.

Claire immediately screamed, 'IT'S FATE, IT'S

FATE, WE'VE GOT THE SAME BIRTHDAY, IT'S FATE!' I just smirked at her but instantly felt embarrassed that I didn't know it was his birthday. I sent him a birthday text to which he replied 'Thank you.' What the fuck is going on in my head? What am I doing? I can't get involved with housemates! PLUS he probably don't even like me like that anyway! There were too many thoughts running a round in my head. *What do I do?* Forget about it and focus on my job or casually text him the following week asking if he wants to go for a drink? I'M NOT GOOD AT THIS. Fuck it, I'll just let it play out. A few weeks passed and I hadn't heard much from Dan. A few texts here and there, that's all. By this point we were a week or so into the summer *Celebrity* series. I couldn't put it off any longer. I texted him to ask if he wanted to go for a drink and he agreed.

We ended up going to a small restaurant on the outskirts of Brentwood that was pretty empty, because I had to be careful we weren't seen together. We had a really nice time and just talked for hours. I knew I liked him and I could tell he liked me. The following night we went to see James at his house with Katy, Michelle and Kelly. We were sat in the garden for only a few short hours when I checked my Twitter to see that his neighbour had tweeted that 'Rylan and Dan from *Big Brother* are in next door's garden ☺ I couldn't even go round to my mate's house without it ending up on Twitter. I was worried people might pick up on it but she only had a few followers so no one did.

Later that week Dan asked if I wanted to pop to his mum's for lunch – bit of a big step but I decided to go. I walked into his mum's garden to be greeted by a table full of people. His son Cameron, mum Wendy, dad Steve, brothers Mark and Chris, their partners Nicola and Fran, and his mum's friends Colin and Jayne. It was a bit awkward to begin with, the odd silence here and there, but everyone seemed pleasant and welcoming. If there was any ice to break, it was well and truly broken when Jayne said the following: 'So what's all this about your teeth then?' Dan's mum Wendy's jaw hit the floor and in a rage she shouted, 'NO, I TOLD YOU YOU WERE NOT ALLOWED TO BRING UP THE TEETH!' I couldn't stop laughing; she was genuinely mortified.

The final of *Celebrity Big Brother* was fast approaching. My management called me to say that a story was coming out about me and Dan. My heart sank. I didn't know the ins and outs, but all I knew is that they were running a front-page story saying me and Dan were together. That evening at midnight I was out of my contract with *Big Brother* as it was the end of the series. At one minute past midnight the story broke online. The *Daily Star* headline was 'RYLAN'S SECRET ROMP WITH *BIG BRO* STAR'. I was horrified. They made out that we'd been seeing each other behind his ex's back, which wasn't true, *and* I'm sure they even claimed we were having it off in the diary room. It couldn't have been more untrue, but the damage was done. Now everyone knew. The following day my big boss Nick called me and asked if it was true. I didn't know what to say – maybe he wouldn't renew my contract for next year because of it, but I couldn't lie to him. He trusted me enough to give me my dream job. I might be about to lose it but . . .

'Yeah, Nick, I'm seeing him. I really like him and I'm so sorry you've found out like this.'

He asked me, 'Are you happy with him?'

I replied, 'Yeah, I am.' He paused for a bit. I dreaded what he was about to say. YOU'RE FIRED! in his best Alan Sugar voice.

'OK, well, if you're happy then I'm happy – don't make a big deal about it and all will be forgotten.'

The biggest weight was lifted from my shoulders. He continued to tell me how proud he was of how I'd done over the summer. It was exactly what I needed to hear.

The hardest thing about stories like that coming out is that you have no control over what is actually said, without doing an interview yourself. Contrary to popular belief, I HATE INTERVIEWS. I like the papers and mags to read in the doctor's surgery like everyone else, but I hate being in them. I didn't want that type of relationship that was plastered over every glossy mag saying 'Rylan and lover have a bath,' 'Rylan and Dan go to the shop,' 'Rylan broken-hearted over Dan supporting Tottenham.' It's all bollocks – I hate it. I was just relieved that we didn't have to hide anymore, and more relieved that Dan wasn't interested in that type of life. He hated it as much as I did. I knew we'd work well.

I started doing more on *This Morning*, presenting 'The Hub' and doing showbiz items. It was nice they took that risk with me and I will for ever be grateful to them for doing so. It became my second regular job. I finally felt lucky to have a good balance when it came to work and personal life. I'd only been dating Dan for a few months, but I felt so comfortable with him and with my work life.

Late September it was my nan's eighty-seventh birthday. All of the family came together and we took her out to a restaurant near the care home she was staying in. She had gotten a bit worse so we'd had to move her into another home a few weeks before where she could have even more attentive care. It was such a lovely night, seeing my nan with her kids, her grandchildren and her great-grandchildren, all together in the same room. That hadn't happened for a long time. I had a photo taken with her and my mum. Part of me worried that it could be our last time together – by now she was quite frail and didn't fully understand what was going on. It meant so much for us all to be together. I've had a lot of time to think about our time together and I think my nan knew what was going on as a few times she cracked a little smile and laughed. I just adored her.

I planned to have a big birthday party to celebrate my twenty-fifth a month later, and we certainly did! Everyone came, all my friends, family, ex-housemates, the *X Factor* lot, it was great. It was the first time Dan met a lot of my family. He had already met my immediate family but I don't think he realised just how big my family was. Me and Claire got up and sang 'Summer of Love' by Steps, old Gina from *Heartbeat* belted out a few, and I think Razor even treated us to a tune or two.

That Christmas I felt content. I had a boyfriend, I knew I was returning to *Big Brother*, I was working on *This Morning* – everything was looking good. The only thing that bothered me was that I still didn't like going anywhere in public. Dan noticed it quite early on. He would suggest going out to a restaurant and I would always persuade him to cook. Whenever we did go out we were never left alone. It's incredibly flattering, but at the same time if I go out to dinner with my boyfriend I don't want half the restaurant coming up to me every five minutes. The attention started to bother Dan as well so he got used to us staying in. My life soon became: go to work, come home, go to work. There was no in-between. I didn't go out for drinks, out to dinner, out to clubs. Whenever I did, I could never be Ross. The second I left my front door I also left him behind and I had no choice but to be Rylan. Rylan can deal with it. Ross can't. I just worked and then went home, but that suited me. Plus, why would I want to go out? I've got Dan waiting for me at home – that was more than enough for me. I knew I needed to address the situation but I was too busy to let it bother me as much as it probably should have.

In January of 2014 I returned to *Celebrity Big Brother*. This time I was the only host of the show as AJ didn't return. I was extremely nervous to take the reins but ultimately I knew I could do it. People began to see that I had become quite good at hosting the show and the teeth jokes had started to die down. I became a full-time presenter of 'The Hub' on *This Morning* and they really helped me build my part on the show. I'd do early mornings on ITV and late nights on Channel 5. I got into the routine quite easily. The year was shaping up to be a great one.

Dan and me were living at my mum's house and I felt it was time to start my own new life and invest my well-earned money and buy a house. We could have gone anywhere, to be honest, but I wanted to stay close to my mum in case she needed me for anything. I worried that if she wasn't well and I was too far away, I wouldn't be able to get to her in time if something happened. Also, I still wanted her to do my ironing – so swings and roundabouts.

We started looking at properties but couldn't seem to find anywhere we liked. One afternoon my cousin Kimberley came round and we decided to go for a little drive to look at what type of house I'd like. Literally two roads away from my mum's I see a house for sale. It was quite dated but also a nice size with a lovely drive. We jumped out of the car and knocked on the door. A lovely French woman answered the door – she told us that the house had just been put up for sale and if we wanted to arrange a viewing to contact the estate agent. The whole time she was talking to me she probably thought I was the rudest person on the planet because my eyes were all over the shop, trying to scope out the layout and the size of the garden I could see through the kitchen window. Me and Dan booked a viewing. Instinctively I could see what could be done in there. It was very dated, but a little-known fact is that I've always fancied myself as a bit of an architect. My fascination for architecture started when I was really young and I would jump on the number 25 bus from Stepney Green to go up the West End with my mum. We would always pass the Lloyd's building on Leadenhall Street in London. I was enchanted by it. The whole concept of the building was 'inside outside'.

The glass elevators and pipes and staircases were on the outside of the building. I was fascinated. One Saturday, late in the evening, one of my cousin's friends who was a security guard at the building let me and my brother go and have a look round the building. It was incredible. I was hooked. Anyway, back to the story. I persuaded Dan we should get the house. Dan's never been too good at things like that and he was a bit apprehensive. I'm quite persuasive, especially when it comes to things I want so I convinced him and I made an offer for the full asking price. It was accepted and we had the keys by the beginning of March.

We completely gutted the place, keeping only the original fireplace. I had a team of around thirty people working on the property from the get-go as I wanted to move in as soon as possible. One afternoon my mum and Auntie Sue took my nan out of the care home for the day and brought her round to my new house. It was still a building site at the time, but I was chuffed she came round. Even though she wasn't with it much, she knew that it was my house and gave me a small smile acknowledging she was pleased for me.

A few weeks later I noticed that my mum started

getting quite defensive. I've lived with her my whole life and I think she was finding it hard to come to terms with the fact that I was finally leaving. Bearing in mind I was moving *around the corner*, she was still finding it hard. Two weeks before the moving date I had a massive argument with my mum. It was terrible. I stormed out and Dan followed me round to the new house, which wasn't ready to move into. I just needed to get out of my mum's. An hour later my mum turned up with black bin liners full of our clothes and left them on the drive. Believe me, you don't want to argue with me or my mum! This went on for a couple of months. We finally moved into our new home, but it was tainted by the fact that we still weren't speaking to my mum. Now, me and my mum are the *most* stubborn people you could ever meet. I wasn't going to make the first move and neither was she. It's clear now that she was just finding the thought of me leaving home hard, but at the time I couldn't see her point and just wanted her to be happy for me.

One afternoon I went to visit my nan at the home. I was shocked to see how much she had deteriorated in a matter of days. She was lying in her bed, refusing to eat or drink anything, and she hadn't spoken to anyone for two weeks. It completely broke me to see her like that. My beloved nan lying there looking so frail and helpless, like a child. I asked Dan to leave me on my own with her because I hated him seeing me upset. I sat on her bed holding her hand, crying and pleading for her to look at me, but nothing. It was like she wasn't even in the room; this is how she'd been behaving for the past few weeks. I laid my head on her chest and sobbed even harder. I just kept pleading with her to speak to me, asking her to say anything. I was trying so hard to remember what the last words she said to me were and I couldn't. It was making me really mad. I finally gave up. I just rested my head on her chest in silence.

Then, out of nowhere, it just happened. It was like someone looked down and gave her three seconds of sanity. I felt her grab my hand, and softly she uttered, 'I love ya.'

And that was it. She went back to how she had been. Relieved, I squeezed her hand and told her I loved her too, thanking her for telling me that. I sat with her for another hour just holding her hand and stroking her face. Sort of knowing, but, without sounding horrible, hoping that it would be the last time I saw her. She wasn't going to get any better, and to know that the last time I saw her she told me she loved me was what anyone would want in those circumstances. I kissed her on the forehead, told her I loved her one last time, and left the room. The following Sunday evening I decided enough was enough with my mum, and drove round to her house. We made up and both agreed to forget about the past couple of months. That evening I went to bed with a clear mind.

At 4 a.m. the phone rang. My beautiful Nanny Rose had passed away in her sleep early that morning, Monday 7 July 2014, aged eighty-seven.

I know she waited to make sure me and my mum made up before she went. I miss her so much.

Later that morning, after a few hours of hazy sleep, I went downstairs to make a tea. I spoke to my mum on the phone who was already at the care home with my Auntie Sue and Auntie Pat. They were dealing with the undertakers and sorting out all the other arrangements. It all felt like a bit of a blur. Dan was with me and did his best to console me. That evening I was due to present *Big Brother* and Dan suggested that I take the day off work. I hadn't taken a day off work since the day I started.

I thought about it long and hard. I went and had a cigarette in the garden and tried to work out if I could actually go to work and do the job. I thought about my nan and how she'd worked her whole life and never gave up. And then I remembered the words she said to me: 'Work as hard as you can because there's always someone else who's waiting to jump in and take it away from you.' I went to work.

That afternoon I arrived at *Big Brother* and pulled Rich aside and told him what had happened. He told me to go home but I refused. That night I presented the show like nothing had happened. Once the show was over, that's when I felt it for the first time. Anyone can say what they want about me but that night I proved myself to myself. I knew if I could host a show after losing my nan, I was in the right job, and – most of all – she would have been so proud of me.

We held the funeral a couple of weeks later. Funerals in my family are always such lovely occasions. To some that might sound strange, but the joke among us is, funerals tend to be more fun than weddings! It was perfect, a sunny day, our entire family, half of East London, the works. The sheer volume of people that couldn't even get into the crematorium just went to show how loved my nan really was.

We held the reception in the ballroom at Orsett Hall in Essex and I booked a Rat Pack singer to come and perform as it was my nan's favourite music. People had a little dance and a sausage roll. Just what my nan would have wanted. Afterwards I invited all of my immediate family back to my house for drinks. It was lovely having everyone round for the first time. We laughed, cried and laughed some more. The night ended with my cousin Karen doing her famous Tina Turner routine dressed in a black bin bag. Just how all our family parties come to a close. Nanny Rose had the send-off she deserved. Deep down I know she was there with us, singing away, rolling out the barrel as she went. She was loved by everyone and is equally missed by each of us. Heaven won't know what's hit it. I know she's up there with all of her brothers and sisters, putting the world to rights and looking after us all down here. We miss you, Nan. You'll always be with us.

'I've not fucking slept for the last two years'

Rylan Ross Clark 2014

18

One year on, and Dan's birthday was looming. I thought it would be nice to surprise him and book a three-day trip to Paris. I'd never been before but he had and said that he really liked it there. I managed to somehow keep it a surprise until a few days before. I'd booked us into a beautiful five-star hotel in the city centre, making sure we had a suite with a view of the Eiffel Tower. If you're gonna go, you've got to do it properly!

On the first day we did the usual touristy things: the Eiffel Tower, the Arc de Triomphe, the Louvre, etc. The following day we decided to visit the bridge in Paris where lovers leave a padlock inscribed with their initials chained to it. I like little things like that – at the end of the day it's an overpriced B&Q padlock you could have probably bought for two quid, but because you're in Paris and it's romantic you're somehow persuaded into parting with ten euros. Thieving bastards. I wrote our initials on the padlock (because I've got better handwriting) and chained it to the railing on the bridge. We both made a wish and threw the key into the Seine. It was a really lovely moment. As I walked away and headed across the bridge to the riverbank, Dan called me. 'Come here,' he said with an awkward grin on his face.

'*Wot?!*' I shouted back to him, sounding as common as anything.

He asked me to walk back over to him. Something in my belly didn't feel right . . . Is he going to do what I think he's going to do? He'd always said that if I wanted to get married I'd have to ask him as it didn't bother him too much, and I'd always said he needed to be the one to propose – it was a bit of a long-running joke. My belly was going round more times than Pete Burns managed to spin in the 1980s. I shouted back at him, 'Fuck off and come on! I want to go see Notre-Dame. For fuck's sake hurry up!'

I think I just got a bit scared. I'd waited my whole life for someone to propose to me and live the dream, and right when I thought someone was about to do it, I go and tell them to fuck off. Smooth, babe, smooth. We walked towards this little row of parks and sat on a bench to have a bottle of water. He kept on sort of hinting for me to stand up or move closer or something – it was all a bit weird. I could feel the word vomit bubbling up inside me. Like a woman possessed, I couldn't help it.

'JUST FOR THE RECORD, if you're gonna propose to me, don't you DARE do it in public. I'd fucking hate it. It's muggy!'

I couldn't physically believe the words had left my mouth. He just laughed it off and said that he wasn't going to propose. Clearly I'd started overreacting for nothing. Standard.

We'd read that the Eiffel Tower sparkles on the hour every hour for five minutes between 7 p.m. and 1 a.m. I was keen to catch it from our balcony that evening, as we hadn't noticed it the night before. We arrived back at the hotel at around 9.15. I jumped in the shower to get ready to head out to dinner, but making sure I'd be ready by 10 to catch the light show. We hadn't planned any-where to eat so were just going to wing it.

Dan had suggested that we visit the Latin Quarter in

Paris as there were some really well-reviewed restaurants around the area. I managed to get ready by 9.55, making sure not to miss the tower sparkle. I pitched up on the balcony with my camera like I was about to witness a royal wedding. I was so excited. After what seemed like for ever, 10 p.m. finally came and the tower sparkled like an upside-down ice-cream cone filled with lit-up glitter and caramel. It was fucking beautiful. I kept screaming at Dan to get out on the balcony as I wanted to get a picture of the both of us with it sparkling in the background. I could hear him fumbling around in the room trying to put a song on his phone. 'Give me your phone,' he said quite abruptly. He took my phone and played our song, Sébastian Tellier, 'La Ritournelle'. I thought he'd done it because it was our song, it was French, we were in France, but that wasn't why. Little did I realise – because I was so engrossed looking through the lens of my camera trying to get a shot of the sparkles – that he was down on one knee with a ring in his hand. I looked at him like he'd just told me he had seconds to live. We were on the seventh floor, my jaw was in the basement . . .

'Ross, I love you. Will you marry me?'

(Me looking like I've had a small stroke.)

'Ross?' he laughed

(Still stroke face.)

'Ross?!'

I replied like any person nervously popping the question would wish . . .

'FUCK OFF, CUNT, CUNT, YOU'RE A CUNT!' And then I hit him in the arm.

Seriously, this is exactly how it happened. He didn't know what to say and neither did I. I was just in so much shock that he had done it. I'd had the near-miss earlier and he'd completely dismissed it when I'd questioned him about it.

'Am I on Ant and Dec? *Is this a wind-up?'*

He looked at me and smiled nervously, saying no. I sort of blocked out everything else. I know it took me an hour to really come around to the idea because the Eiffel Tower started to sparkle again. Of course I said yes, and we took a photo with the Eiffel Tower sparkling in the distance.

We jumped in a cab and headed to the Latin Quarter. We asked the taxi driver to recommend a restaurant and he dropped us outside a typical French bistro. We went in and sat down and were given the menu. I couldn't understand a word of it and they didn't have an English translation. I tried working out what dishes were served and I think I made out 'fillet of duck foot with toenail jus and snail faeces'. I wasn't going to like it. We made our excuses, embarrassed to up and leave. I think I put on a little act that there was an emergency and we hurried out.

Next door was the Emporio Armani Caffé – that sounds like a bit of me, I like a good Italian. Fully booked. Fuck's sake. Over the road was a nice-looking restaurant called something along the line of 'Bogies'. Seriously. It had tables available and we went for it. We sat down and the typically rude waiter pushed us to make a quick choice as the kitchen was about to close. We both went for the chicken. Can't go wrong with a bit of chicken. We ordered a bottle of red wine and waited patiently for our food. To the left of us was a table of around six French people. They were laughing and joking and seemingly having a great night. I did the standard nod and smile, showing off my ring . . . engagement ring, I should clarify, and sat there feeling like Queen Latifah. Our food showed up and looked less than appetising. All I could describe it as was a chicken foot with twelve bones hanging out of it – it most definitely wasn't my cup of tea. I didn't want to put a bad spin on the night so I attempted to eat it. A few minutes later I felt something on my foot. I looked underneath the table to find a rat sat next to my shoe. A FUCKING RAT, MATE! I jumped out of my chair and out of my skin and screamed. The rat did a runner. I looked around at the table of French friends who were seemingly unconcerned at the fact that there was a rat in the restaurant. I was sort of looking to them to be as outraged as I was, but they seemed casual. Wrong'uns. Anyway, Dan didn't see it and thought I was overreacting so for some random fucking reason I decided to try and carry on eating my food. Two minutes later the same thing happened again, only this time Dan saw it as well. We both jumped up and both looked over to the table of French friends for some shared disgust at what had happened. Once again they took it in their stride. I couldn't help but think that the sort of people who were eating in Restaurant Bogie weren't the sort of people I'd like to be hanging about with. The rude waiter finally came over after what seemed like five minutes' worth of screams, and we informed him what had happened. His response was priceless . . .

'Well, sir,' (at least he didn't say '*madame*') 'this is an old city, and we have a metro, so you know, these things will happen.'

I looked at him, I looked at Dan, I looked back at him and replied, 'Well, mate, we come from London, we've got the Underground, and if a rat ran over my foot in a restaurant there it would be shut down – SHUT DOWN, I TELL YOU!'

He genuinely couldn't give a fuck and went back to doing what he was doing. We both couldn't stay there, it was vile, so we decided to leave. I threw 100 euros down on the table and went to leave. 'Don't fucking pay for it,' Dan shouted at me. I just felt embarrassed. The table of French friends was giving me evils by this point and I just wanted to get out of there. Dan walked back over to the table and grabbed the bottle of wine, 'Well, if you're paying for it, I'm fucking taking this,' he said assertively. Fair dos.

So there we were, on our magical engagement night, walking the streets of Paris with a half-drunk bottle of red wine and rat piss on my Louboutins. We jumped into a taxi and asked the driver to take us to the McDonald's on the Champs-Elysées. He was a nice French man called

Sammy. We told him that we had got engaged and what had happened at the restaurant. He then informed us that Restaurant Bogies had only just been reopened. Apparently it had been shut down by health and safety for 'poor hygiene', and people had spotted, in Sammy's words, 'bery bery big rats' (he actually pronounced it like that). WE WEREN'T ALONE! We were both fuming that our engagement night was about to finish up in McDonald's but by that point we were damaged and hungry. Sammy dropped us at the doors of McDonald's. I'd never been more happy to see the Golden Arches in my life. I walked up to the doors and was greeted by a man who I believed was a porter. You know, they're quite fancy in France and all that. He wasn't. He was a security guard. Rather than opening the door for me like I expected him to, he put his arm across it and blocked my way. 'Too many people, no entry,' he snarled. Is this fucking arsehole taking the piss? There were about eight people queuing up.

By this point I was completely done, and didn't give a fuck. I dropped to my knees in rat-piss-soaked Louboutins on my ENGAGEMENT NIGHT and pleaded with a French bouncer to let me in none other than

MC-FUCKING-DONALD'S. I only wanted a double cheeseburger, for fuck's sake. Anyone would have thought I was asking to buy his liver on the black market! He stood there very stern and refused to let me in. I just saw red and did the ultimate celeb faux pas, for the first and quite potentially last time in my life. 'DON'T YOU KNOW WHO I AM?! IF THIS WAS IN BRITAIN, BELIEVE ME, I'D BE ABLE TO GET INTO ANY FUCK-ING MCDONALD'S I WANT!' That told him. If fell on deaf ears and I was finally defeated. Sammy dropped us both back at our hotel. We ordered a croque monsieur on room service and fell asleep before even finishing it. How fucking romantic. Calling my now-fiancé a cunt, punch-ing him, leaving one restaurant, refused entry to another, eating in a place called Bogies, two 'BERY BIG' rats, refused entry to McDonald's, and no nookie. Who says romance is dead?

The following day it was time to go home. I was a little bit frightened about wearing the engagement ring, because 1: it was slightly too big and I was worried I'd lose it, and 2: it only takes one person to take one photo and everyone will know I'm engaged. I didn't want that. The *last* thing I wanted was for people I didn't know to find out I was engaged before we had told all our friends and family. I decided not to wear it for the journey home, which was quite lucky as a few people asked for photos at Gare du Nord station in Paris. Both me and Dan had called our mums the night before and told them what had happened. They were both over the moon. We didn't know what to do about telling everyone else. It's not the fact we didn't trust people around us, but sometimes things about me would come out in the press that only a few close friends and family knew about, and it definitely worried us. I wasn't ready to make it public. In fact in an ideal world we would be able to keep it between us for as long as possible, but we knew eventually it would have to come out, and when it did we wanted it to be under our control.

I started back at *Celebrity Big Brother* a week later. It was so hard not to tell the people that had become like family to me my news. I can't stress enough how working with the team on a daily basis brings you all so close together, and keeping something this big from them was hard. They're like my second family. The problem was I hadn't told all of my first and real family, so I wasn't going to risk it. We decided to tell strictly our close family and some friends. Everyone was so happy for us. We asked everyone to keep the news to themselves and they all respected our wishes. Unfortunately, a short while after our family announcement it was out in the press and public domain. Something I really didn't want to happen. It killed me that I was getting texts from my cousins asking if I was engaged – I found it fucking embarrassing. We decided that the best way to deal with it was to send a tweet with a photo and confirm we were engaged, as we'd rather it came from us.

It bothered me so much that something we'd tried to keep so private had suddenly became so public without us knowing how. And something else had been bothering me recently with one of my friends. I noticed that James had been hanging around with a few of the people that supported me on Twitter in real life and I found it slightly odd. I'm not saying that there was anything wrong with it, and believe me, as much as I hate the word 'fans' because it sounds muggy, I'm going to have to use it. I'd seen that he was hanging around with some of them in his personal time, i.e. not when he came to see me at work, where they would be outside the studio waiting for photographs. Personally I was made up that all

293

my 'Sirens', as they've named themselves, liked James and got on well with him when they saw him at work with me or spoke to him on Twitter, but, as you probably know by now, I like to have a line between my work and personal life, and James was very much part of my personal life, for the last fourteen years to be precise.

It all started when I noticed that he was going to visit one of the girls and her mum up north at their home. My best friend travelling miles to stay with one of my fans in her home with her mum. That's how I see it. Black and white. As much as I adore the people that support me, I found it really weird that my BEST FRIEND was sleeping in their house. I didn't understand it. I still don't. The Sirens would always send me gifts and things and I would always tell them not to as they were mostly around the ages of 14/15 and I didn't want young girls spending their money on me. Then I started to see James tweeting thank you for gifts he had received from them and again I found that strange. Of course I understand with him being my best mate the girls may send him things or cards, but it was starting to become quite excessive. I raised the issue with a couple of our mutual friends, asking them if they thought it was weird or not. They didn't really know what to say; they were aware of what was going on but sort of brushed it off and tried to justify it.

So this continued behaviour had been making me uncomfortable for months, and as time went on I found it difficult to broach the subject with him. Towards the middle of *Celebrity Big Brother*, Ben came up to my dressing room and told me that he had just spotted James outside the studios having photos done with some of the Sirens, who would normally come down to see me before and after the show at the gates. I found it doubly odd because I didn't know James was coming to see the show in the first place. I presumed he must've wanted it to be a surprise for me, so I didn't text him and carried on getting ready to present the show. I decided I would put my best acting on if I spotted him in the audience. I walked into the studio to amazing applause from the ever-so-loyal *Bit on the Side* audience, but there was a problem. I couldn't see James. I didn't understand why he wasn't there. I walked over to Wendy who works at *Big Brother* – she's the one who sorts out the audience tickets. James had her number as I had introduced them before and I was sure he'd contacted her about coming down secretly and she had sorted it out for him. At this point I thought maybe he was sat in the office or something. I asked her if he was in the building. She had no idea what I was going on about. I presented the rest of the show and an hour later left the studios. As I left, a few of the Sirens were there at the gate to greet me and ask for photos. I recognised one of them and asked her if she had seen James.

'Yeah, we all went to Harvester for dinner. It was so lovely.'

I didn't know what to say. What do you say? All I could think is that my long-standing *best friend* of fourteen years is no more than ten yards away from my dressing room, having travelled at least forty-five minutes to get here, and hasn't even texted me to tell me he's here! What the fuck is going on? Am I going mad or is this weird? I sort of tried to forget about it and put it down as a one-off. The following week it happened again. One afternoon I strolled into work and Wendy told me James had been in contact to get two tickets for finale week. Again I found it strange that he hadn't contacted me to ask to come down as he normally did, but this time I just thought maybe he didn't want to bother me as it was finale week and he knew it was going to be mega-busy.

No. There's two types of ticket for my show. There's the general audience ticket where you apply on the website, arrive at a certain time and wait at security to be brought into the bar and checked off, have a few drinks, get escorted into the studio and watch the show, have a lovely night and then go home. Then there are my tickets, for friends of mine, where you turn up whatever time you want, and your name would be waiting at the security desk along with a security pass that gives you access to my dressing room, the office, studio, etc. An access-all-areas, if you like. Something that James and any of my friends would have when they visited me at *Big Brother*. He had asked for two tickets for that night. There was one problem: they weren't for him. They were for two girls who followed me on Twitter, who in all honesty were lovely but now had direct access to my dressing room as 'guest's of mine. This seriously pissed me off. I'm fiercely private and I could easily have not known anything about it. I doubt I would have been stabbed or anything, but I could have walked naked out of my dressing-room shower!

I didn't have the heart to tell Wendy to cancel the tickets. I told her simply to swap lists and look after them but not to give them security passes. They had a good night. Throughout that whole show I couldn't shake off what was happening. He's pally-pally with young girls and their parents and now he's getting my followers tickets to my show – what the fuck is going on? I didn't know how to handle the situation. It had been bothering me for months and still I didn't know what to say.

A week or so later I was speaking to another friend of mine who does a similar job to me. I confided in her about not knowing how to handle the situation. She told me that she had gone through something similar and that I *had* to talk to him about it. Even with her advice I still kept putting it off.

On 3 October I wasn't prepared for the text I woke up to from James. I looked at the message which was sent very early that morning and laughed. I presumed he'd had a heavy night out and had sent it to me by mistake. I replied saying, 'You've sent this to me, babe.'

It quickly became apparent that he'd meant to send it to me – he told me he'd heard that I had spoken to a friend of mine and was under the impression that I was slagging him off. She'd casually mentioned it to two of her other mates in the pub when they'd asked how I was, and gossip got twisted and made to sound worse. I knew I had to explain exactly what I'd said. I said that I didn't understand why he was hanging about with these girls and that I found it strange since my personal and work lives are two separate things, and I was finding it hard to understand. I wasn't rude in the slightest; in fact I think I was being as sensitive as I could.

He then wrote me a long message to say that I was being selfish, and that I had let it all go too much to my head. Accusing me of becoming someone that thinks they're above everyone and everything. There was too much stuff that he listed that I can't even go into right now, but it hurt. The bit that got me was the suggestion that I'd been a bad friend, who seemingly now he's in the public eye was ignoring calls and not turning up for social dos. It read like a scene from a really bad film. And I didn't want to be in it. I felt my jaw drop. I couldn't believe what I was reading. I started to question every-thing. Not just things in recent years but all the time that we'd spent growing up together. Have I really been a bad friend? What have I done? I started crying and it all got too much for me. I sat on the bed staring at the floor in disbelief. There was one thing that really bothered me though. He said that the family he'd visited in Liverpool all thought I was a prick. Well, with all due respect, I don't think I'd put myself out and travel up to Liverpool to spend time with a family who thought my BEST FRIEND was a prick. That's what bothered me, as I knew he had been visiting them for months. This is someone who knows EVERYTHING about me, and I know EVERYTHING about him. Have I really driven him to this? Is this the price of doing what I love? Instantly I wished I wasn't famous. I wished I had never gone to that very first *X Factor* audition. None of this would have happened and nothing would have changed. I really beat myself up over it.

I then started to get angry. Who the fuck is he, saying those things to me? I'VE DONE NOTHING FUCKING WRONG to him or anyone for that matter. I didn't deserve it. Granted I've missed social occasions because I don't have a nine-to-five job and my work hours vary. Granted I don't always answer my phone, but I try to call or text back when I can. Granted I missed his birthday party because I already said I'd go to my cousin's fortieth, and anyway he only told me about it a week before. BUT THAT DOES'T JUSTIFY IT. How fucking dare he say I don't 'graft' for a living and just got lucky? *I've not fucking slept for the last two years.* I've given myself fucking insecurities and agoraphobia just to make my life better and make a good living for myself. There are so many things that upset me about what he said. But I'm going to leave it there. I don't need or want to defend myself. He has every right to say what he said as it's his opinion and I respect that. I also have every right to have my opinion on what was bothering me regarding him. The reason I've put this in the book isn't to make a scene, not to single him out, but because he has been one of the biggest parts of my life, and I couldn't not put it in. Fans would tweet me and ask why James wasn't around. I never had the heart to say 'Because he thinks I'm a cunt' to a twelve-year-old. But mainly because I'm gutted, and I want people to know whatever they think might have happened, in my eyes, this is what happened. That was the day I lost the best friend I ever had.

'We had a cuddle and looked at each other knowing this is what we both wanted'

Rylan Ross Clark 2015

19

Moving towards Christmas, it was time to talk wedding. Me and Dan had decided we wanted to get married in November 2015. By this point I had signed with James Grant Group as my management. They are the best in the business, it was a fucking honour to be asked to join them and I was so grateful. My new manager was Jack Madeley. Yep, that's right, MADELEY. *Richard and Judy are his mum and dad*. If you're gonna be managed by anyone, I mean, come on – RICHARD AND FUCKING JUDY. He was amazing, he knew what I wanted to do and, more importantly, he knew what I COULD do. I was engaged, and my career was on the up. Things couldn't be better. This was our first Christmas in our own home and we decided to have all our immediate family over for the holidays. Finally I felt like an adult, cooking a turkey (Jamie Oliver sent me one. Cheers, Jamie, it was lovely), having a beverage or two, opening presents, a few arguments, all in the comfort of my own home. It really was the first time in my life I *really* felt settled. It went so well we decided to have New Year's at our house as well, and most of my family and friends came. I couldn't help thinking about James. It had been over two months since we last spoke and normally we were always together for New Year – well, literally every New Year since we were about fourteen. I very nearly texted him. But I held myself back. The following morning I received a text from him wishing me happy New Year. I didn't know what to do. Is he pissed? Did he mean to send it to me? Maybe. I just sent back a kiss and left it at that. Nothing else came through and I decided to forget about it.

The year 2015 was shaping up to be a great one for me. Not only did I have *Big Brother*, two series of *Celebrity Big Brother*, *This Morning* and other hosting gigs, but I had also been asked to take part in *Celebrity MasterChef*. Ohhhhhhh, DO ME A FAVOUR. I'm no Ainsley Harriott – the only thing we've got in common is we both like a boogie in the kitchen, but that's where the similarities pretty much stopped. I decided to turn it down. After a few more calls from Jack I insisted it just wasn't for me. I'd worked so hard over the past two and a half years to become a presenter and not a reality star that I didn't want to fall back into it. Dan agreed with me.

After what seemed like months I asked old Linda. She loved a bit of *MasterChef* and without a second's thought she said it would be a great idea. I should do it. I think her exact words were 'Fucking do it.' All right, Lin, calm yourself. I finally decided that I should do it. After all, what's the worst that could happen?

Before starting *Celebrity MasterChef*, me and Dan flew to New York for a few days for a little holiday. It was a well-earned break as we had both been so busy. One night in the hotel, whilst getting ready for dinner, I received a text. It was from James. He told me that his sister had given birth and because it was the first time he had become an uncle, and because I was an uncle to Harvey and Olivia, he wanted to text me. It didn't really make sense but I could see what he meant. I felt like shit. It was so sad. I'd been part of their family and Louise, his sister, had been like my family for the last fourteen years; now she'd had her baby and I didn't even know about it. What do I do? Just forget about it and be best mates again? It felt wrong not knowing the answer to that question. It broke me a bit. But even though it did I made a tough decision that day. I still couldn't believe what had happened For now and without being rude, decided that I didn't want to speak to him. I texted him back offering my sincere congratulations to Louise and told him to be a good uncle. He replied almost instantly, saying 'You really don't like me, do you?' I didn't reply. If you don't have anything nice to say, then don't say anything. I enjoyed the rest of my break and flew back to London.

It was time for me to put my culinary skills to the test on national TV's most gruelling cooking competition. I arrived at 3 Mills Studios in Bow. I was a little early and decided to head over to where the original Big Brother house used to be. I remembered back to clothes-peg day with fond memories, looking around and realising how far I had come from back then. How the fuck I managed to do it I'll never know, but that was a bit of a light-bulb moment. Fuck that though, I ain't got time for strolls down Memory Lane – it's time to get cooking.

I walked into the *Celebrity MasterChef* kitchen along-side Arlene Phillips, Kimberly Wyatt, Andy Akinwolere and Craig Gazey. We all hit it off straight away, but unfortunately there was no time for fun and games. Almost instantly we were thrown into the deep end with a pressure test. Gregg Wallace and John Torode entered the kitchen and told us we only had one hour to make whatever we wanted using only the ingredients found on our table. There was a fucking fish with a face still on it and what looked like someone's inner thigh casually lying across the sideboard. 'Your one hour begins now. *Let's cook!*' John exclaimed.

I looked at the fish, confused what to do.

The fish looked back at me, confused why the fuck I was on the show.

I looked at the human thigh lying on the side, then looked again and realised it was someone's or something's liver.

I looked around to see everyone had already started.

I looked at the clock and I had forty-five minutes left.

I looked at . . .

WHAT?! HOW THE FUCK HAS FIFTEEN MINUTES GONE ALREADY?! Arlene was already flaming her liver and Kimberly had practically finished her fish. What the fuck am I gonna do here? I started to think what I could do. I could see some biscuits, cream cheese and raspberries. I started to realise that although the other four had all used either the liver or the fish, the judges didn't actually say we *had* to use either of them. Bollocks, I'm gonna make a cheesecake! Only problem is I've *never* made a cheesecake. I knew you had to put butter with the biscuits because people would talk about one of Gregg's favourite catchphrases on the show: 'buttery biscuit base'. I picked up the biscuits and smashed them up to within an inch of their lives. I couldn't work out, though, how to add the butter. I remembered back to school in food technology and my old teacher telling me to 'massage' the butter into it. What my memory failed to tell me was that that technique was for use with flour when making pastry . . .

Fifteen minutes later I was still fucking MASSAGING butter into broken biscuits. I got the odd dirty look from people but I carried on regardless. I turned around and asked Craig and Kimberly what to put in the cream cheese and I got nothing. My luck must have been in as I got 'dish of the day' from the judges. They LOVED IT, and

also thought I was very clever not using the main ingredients. And quite possibly the biggest accolade, Gregg told
me I had a great buttery biscuit base. Over the three
months it took to film *Celebrity MasterChef* I can genuinely say I had a fucking amazing time. I got on great with
all the other contestants: Sheree Murphy, Scott Maslen,
Sam Nixon, Mica Paris, Chesney Hawkes and Tom
Parker. The production team loved us – and hated us (we
were proper naughty). As much as we had fun along the
way, the competition really was hard. I got the usual 'He's
a wanker,' 'Why are they putting this reality Z-lister on
this show?' type of comments from the press and others,
but ultimately I didn't care. I was doing quite well, in fact.
One time I made my own version of a Happy Meal on the
show, because I could. I've always been creative – very
creative, in this case. Because I couldn't find a box big
enough for a Happy Meal, I went to a pet shop and bought
a 'small cat carrier' to put the food in, minus the cat. I
made it to the final three along with Kimberly and Sam.

Kimberly eventually won, leaving me and Sam run-
ners-up. I was so grateful I'd made it that far. When the
series finally aired, a lot of the negative comments on
social media soon became positive. It was the first time

310

I'd really been pushed to a BBC audience and I think the show changed a lot of people's opinions of me. I want to genuinely thank everyone who worked on it for persuading me to do it in the first place.

By the time the show aired it was the month of June. Me and Dan had booked the venue for our wedding, but not much else. I was so busy with *Big Brother* – and Dan was with his work too – that it took a bit of a back seat. We would watch episodes of *Don't Tell the Bride* and see couples organise everything in two weeks for around £12,000. Easy. I wasn't worried in the slightest. By September, when *Celebrity Big Brother* had come to an end, the heat was really on. We had *everything* still to do. One of the things we had decided on was that for our bridesmaids we would only have family and one friend each. We had my sister-in-law Jayne, my cousins Cheryl, Hayley and Kimberley and my niece Olivia. Dan decided to have his two sister-in-laws Fran and Nicola, and his nieces Jessica and Bella. Both of us still had to decide on one friend. Dan decided to choose his friend Hazel. They were in *Big Brother* together and became incredibly close. I didn't really know what to do but deep down I knew who I wanted. I decided I wanted Claire from Steps. We got so close in the Big Brother house and I could always rely on Claire to understand what I was going through. I respected her so much, and she was there at the beginning of me and Dan. Let me just say this, HAVING ELEVEN FUSSY BRIDESMAIDS WAS A FUCKING NIGHT-MARE. I've never had so many discussions of shoes, dress cuts, materials and embellishments. I hadn't even begun to look at what me and Dan were going to wear. As much as they were a nightmare as a group, we love them all and wouldn't have had it any different.

The wedding day was approaching fast. The idea of doing a *Don't Tell the Bride* and organising a quick and cost-effective celebration went well and truly out the window. A month before the wedding we were nearly up to a six-figure sum already. I didn't care at that point. This was my dream wedding. Growing up I always said I wanted the Essex dream – a husband and a Range Rover. I'd bought the Range Rover a few months before so I was halfway there at least.

The week of the wedding finally hit us. We managed to keep it out of the press and public eye. It wasn't until the Wednesday before that we noticed some cars down our road. They had been there for hours with people sitting in them. At first I shat myself thinking I was about to be murdered by an organised criminal gang, but eventually I realised it was paparazzi. I hated it. I've never had them outside my home. I'm not one of those people who rings paps up to tell them where they're going. I'm private. What fucked me off more was the fact that I wasn't selling my wedding. I wasn't getting married to have it in a magazine and earn money, I was getting married because I wanted to show the people I love that I want to spend the rest of my life with the person I'm in love with. For the four days running up to the wedding they didn't leave. This made it incredibly hard to go to the venue and check everything was exactly how I wanted it as I was worried they would follow me. We'd tried to keep the venue and date quiet but someone must have opened their mouth. My suspicions were confirmed when, the day before, the descriptions of our acrylic mirror invites appeared in the press. I've definitely got an idea as to who I think it was, but unfortunately I'll never be able to verify it. I was so adamant that it should not ruin the wedding though. And it didn't.

On the Friday afternoon we made our way to Braxted Park Estate in Essex to start our three-day celebration.

All of the wedding party, bridesmaids, groomsmen, etc., were staying at the venue for the three days with us. That Friday evening we all got together to have a beautiful meal. It all seemed such a blur. I remember that evening slipping outside to the front of the property with Kimberley. We sat there and spoke about what had happened in our lives. We were born about two weeks apart so have always been close from a young age. I think that was the moment, sitting looking over the acres of land under nightfall outside the beautiful manor house we were in that I realised I was *actually* getting married.

After the dinner, the rest of them surprised me and Dan with a book that they had all written special messages in. It was so incredibly beautiful, and each one of them stood up around the table to read out what they had written. That's when I knew that everyone sat in that room was most definitely someone we wanted to share our special day with us. After a few more drinks and putting the world to rights, it was time for bed. Me and Dan headed back to the cottage and went to sleep. I slept surprisingly well that night.

At 8 a.m. I was awake. I quickly ran to the window to check if it was pissing down. It wasn't a seaside sunny spectacular but it wasn't reminiscent of a scene from *Twister* either, so I wasn't too disappointed. Dan said his goodbyes and headed over to the main house where he was going to get ready with his brothers. It was emotional as I knew the next time I would see him we'd be saying our I do's.

The security team had started at 6 a.m. and were patrolling the land making sure no one could get into the venue without crossing the security checkpoint. I stood by the door of my cottage and had a cigarette, watching in awe at their precise movements. It was like something out of a James Bond film. Hazel and Claire came out of their stable rooms and we decided to go for breakfast and meet up with everyone else. Whilst we sat down for breakfast, through the window I could see some of the security members running towards my cottage. I didn't know what the fuck was going on, but my brother jumped out of his seat as if he thought something was very wrong. I walked outside to go and see what the problem was, but was quickly ushered back in by a member of security.

It turns out that overnight one of the paps had broken into the site and, at around 4 a.m., had parked his car alongside all our cars outside the cottage. When security started at 6 a.m. they knew that all the wedding party's cars were parked there, so assumed everything was normal. What they didn't spot – and neither did any of us – was this pap, sitting in the car taking pictures. He was a few feet away from the front door I had graced earlier that morning, make-up-less, having a fag and looking like Dot Cotton. These pictures quickly surfaced online and were in the press within thirty minutes. I felt fucking violated. Not only because I'd spent so much money to keep that from happening, but by the fact that someone would go to such lengths to ruin someone's big day, particularly as I never wanted anyone outside my friends and family to talk about it anyway! If I was one of those people who sold every second of my life to every magazine for a tenner I could understand it, but I wasn't. If I ever go anywhere and someone asks me for a photo I *always* say yes. That's my job and it's part of the package. But to the man who did that, on my wedding day, when you knew full well that I didn't want it or, dare I say, deserve that – FUCK YOU.

I didn't have much time to be upset as I had to get ready. My make-up artist Debbie arrived and started working her magic. She was my make-up artist on *The X Factor* and I'd always say, 'If I ever get famous, I'm taking you with me' – and I did. I never break a promise. She was quite emotional because she knew how much the day meant to me. My mum and Auntie Pat came into the cottage to have a cup of tea with me. They looked beautiful. I could see my mum was nervous but she was trying her best to hide it. I thought she was worried that someone would manage to get into the venue and ruin the day, but in fact the real reason why she was nervous is this.

She had washed her hair earlier in the morning and went to have it blow-dried by my styling team along with the rest of the bridesmaids. Problem was she'd only just realised that she had brought two conditioners with her instead of a shampoo and a conditioner, and so she'd washed *and* conditioned her hair using conditioner, and in her own words was worried that her hair would look 'fucking flat as a pancake'. We had a good laugh about it and she quickly got over it. Go on, Linda.

As I started to get my wedding suit on I could see out the back of my cottage that guests had already started to arrive. My stomach started to turn like I was on a rollercoaster. I wasn't scared of anything, but I just felt weird. The time had finally come to get married. I was walked over to the main house, escorted by the security team under ten white umbrellas – that was to stop anyone getting a picture with a long-lens camera and it worked, but ultimately I'd paid them good money and wanted to feel important. All the guests were seated and it was time to enter the atrium. Waiting in there was the bridal party. The bridesmaids and our groomsmen. Seeing all of them in their beautiful bridal gowns and crisp black suits started to make me emotional. I ran out of the room for a quick cry. It was real, it was in front of me and it was now. Dan walked into the room and looked handsome. We had a cuddle and looked at each other knowing this is what we both wanted.

The music started playing and the bridesmaids and groomsmen walked hand-in-hand down the aisle before us. I took Dan's hand and started to walk. As we entered the orangery, decked with white voile and hundreds of flowers, everyone started to applaud. I could see some familiar faces in the crowd but it was all a total blur.

The ceremony was beautiful, and seeing as we are both partial to a joke, we laughed when the registrar announced Mr and Mrs Clark-Neal. The crowd erupted in laughter as well. She unfortunately wanted the ground to swallow her up, but we told her not to worry. We had done it. We were finally married and ready to spend the rest of our lives together. As you know, I'm quite a private person, so that's all you're getting out of me about the wedding. You could say this is the perfect time to start the next chapter.

All in good time, babe, all in good time.

The moral of my Story

Rylan Clark-Neal 2016

20

When I was nine years old, my sister-in-law Jayne took me and a few of my cousins to the Ragged School Museum. It was a museum up the road from where I lived in Stepney Green that was fitted out like an olden-day school from the 1920s. They put on activities for children in the summer holidays. On arrival we were given a choice of activity. 1: do a treasure hunt around the museum, ticking items off a list, and at the end you could pick a small gift from the gift shop, or 2: take part in an art and craft class and make a small cardboard Victorian box. I, being the greedy kid I was, wanted to do both, but had to choose only one. After contemplating my options I remembered seeing a little pack of 'magic' plastic beans in the gift shop. They were small little plastic tubes with a metal ball bearing inside that made the beans seem like they were jumping around in your hand. I wanted them, so I decided to do the treasure hunt. One of my cousins decided to do it with me and the rest went to do the art and craft class. As excited as I was to finish the treasure hunt and receive my magic bean prize, I couldn't help feeling upset I couldn't also do the craft class. I finished the treasure hunt after around ten minutes and was rewarded with the magic beans. The lady who was looking after us popped her head into the art and craft class then said, 'If you want you can jump in and join them – they've only just started.' I couldn't believe my luck. Not only did I get to do the treasure hunt and get my magic beans, but I also got to leave with my very own hand-crafted cardboard Victorian box. The moral of my story is: don't settle for choosing one or the other. If you really want to do it all, don't let anyone tell you you can't. You can, and some-times you just need to believe you can.

Love Ross x x

Acknowledgements

To my mum – Mum; you've been the biggest headache but the biggest asset anyone could ask for. I need you to know how much I appreciate everything you've done for me over the years. I don't say it enough but I really do appreciate everything. I wouldn't want our relationship to be any different to what it is. Just for fuck's sake stop telling me to put the bins out every Sunday. IT'S MY HOUSE! I KNOW WHEN THE BINS GO OUT! I love you so much and I can't say any more than that x

To my Nanny Rose – My second mum, wherever you are, I know you're always with us all, looking after us. You have been like a second mum to me and not a day goes by that I don't miss you. I hope where you are you're still singing all the old time classics and make sure you bang out a version of 'Roll Out The Barrel' for me. I love you and miss you always x

To Dan – Who would have thought you would marry 'that idiot off *X Factor*' You have changed my life so much and the fact that you've met my family and still agreed to marry me is beyond me. Thank you so much for giving me Cameron and your family to have as part of mine. We're so lucky that our families completely lock together seamlessly. I love you with all my heart and would never hurt you. But if you hurt me . . . I'll cut it off! I'm joking. I love you the world and back and here's to the rest of our lives together. I love you x

To Jamie, Jayne, Harvey and Olivia – Jamie, you've been the Dad I never had and for that I cannot thank you enough. I'm so glad you met Jayne and I love her like a sister. It's so amazing now to be in a position that I can look after Harvey and Olivia like you always looked after me growing up. Thank you for bringing them into this world. Harvey – be good, Olivia – stay away from the boys! x

To Team Rylan – Ben, you are my best friend. Everything we've done over the years will never compare to the friendship we will always have. I love you like a brother and thank you for always being there for me; the early mornings, the late nights and all the in-betweens. I can't thank you enough. Debbie, you're not just my make-up artist your also one of my closest friends. You do SO much for me it's completely unreal. I

324

don't know what I would do without you, but please, stop trying to buy me animals for the garden! Tracey, thanks so much for always tanning/ plucking/waxing/threading and treating me. You've been amazing to me all these years and I can't thank you enough. Rikki, I was so lucky to work with you throughout *X Factor* and now full time. You've always made me look as good as I can and for that you deserve a medal, but babe FIND ME THEM BLACK FUCKING LOUBOUTINS! Hayley, from doing work experience in the salon to eleven years on you still doing my hair. Thanks for always getting rid of my roots and for fuck's sake NEVER use a No.1 on the side of my head again.

Love you ALL so much x

To my family – I've got the best family anyone could ask for. Each and EVERY ONE of you mean so much to me. Thank you for being there for me growing up. My aunts, uncles, cousins, family friends, EVERYONE. I know I was the devil child and always wanted to know everything but it paid off in the end, plus you all get the benefits of it so DON'T START! To all the Neal side of the family, I'm so happy you're all part of my life I wouldn't want it any other way, even when Wendy has too many vodkas!

Love you all x

To my friends – I can't even begin to name you all, YOU know who you are. For those that fell along the way I still hold respect for you. For those that are still here which I can count on one hand I applaud you, you've put up with me this long. Whether it's been twenty years or two years it doesn't matter. I'm lucky to have you around me and to know you're always there when I need you. It's the biggest gift any of you could give me. Thank you x

To my James Grant Family – Well hark at you lot taking on a reality reject! I cannot thank you guys enough, there are about a million of you that work with me and Jesus you all deserve a medal! Neil, Paul, thanks for actually agreeing to take me on. I hope you still stand by that decision! To Rory, a massive thank you for being part of the book, I thoroughly enjoyed working with you – here's to the next one! Sophie, you are my favourite northerner and I apologise for ringing you at silly o'clock because I've forgotten something. George, I loved working with you and I'll miss you dearly! Holly, Best Tits at James Grant Award goes to you. You literally crack me up and I'm so glad to work with you. Finally, Jack – what can I say about you? Thank you for being the best manager anyone could ask for, all I've got for you is four words: YOU SAY WE PAY! Xxx

To "The Book Massive" – So many of you have made this happen at Century, Cornerstone and I can't begin to thank each and every one of you. To Becky, thank you for all your work on the book. I know choosing the pictures were a chore but thanks for letting me have a few extras! Sue, Sue! I know you hate me calling you Sue and I'm the only one who can get away without saying SueSAN! Thank you for believing in me and giving me this opportunity. It means the world and I look forward to a Tate Lunch soon! On your table! Ajda, there are no words to describe my feelings towards you. You have been amazing day in, day out, putting up with my ridiculous OCD requests to change the minutest of things. I couldn't have done this without you. I'm still getting that injunction though, forever my favourite stalker. Love yas x

To my *X Factor* Family – Wherever we are now, whatever we're doing, we fucking done it! And not to start any controversy, but we had a fucking good year! Utmost respect to you all and THANK YOU for making that part of my life easier than it would have been without you all. To all the staff, crew and contestants. Love you all x

To my *Big Brother* Family – To my housemates, you were all part of a little ginger boy's dream-come-true and I wouldn't have wanted to spend it with anyone else. The times we had in that house that would never be shown on TV were always the best and OURS and OURS ALONE to remember. Emma, thank you for looking after me in the early days and always helping me along the way, and thanks for letting me bore you in your dressing room every eviction day while you were trying to get ready. Nick, thanks for the job, Big Boy; you've changed my life and I can never repay you for taking that chance. To all of my fellow crew members at *Big Brother* and *Big Brother's Bit On The Side*, thank you. I couldn't ask for a better team to have around. We make the best show on earth and we know it! BBBOTS! BBBOTS! x

To my *This Morning* Family – To everyone at *This Morning*, THANK YOU for accepting me as part of your amazing family. I never dreamt growing up that I would be a part of such an amazing show that I always watched growing up. You have all been so welcoming of me, even in the early days when I had no fucking idea what I was doing, and for that I'll be forever grateful. I'm honoured to be able to say that I've hosted such an amazing show alongside the likes of Phil and Holly, who have welcomed me so well and always been there to help me, and more importantly, take the piss with me! Tequilas on yous! x

To Ruth and Eamonn – My TV Mum and Dad. I've always admired the pair of you and from the bottom of my heart I fucking adore you both. Too many people in this industry are SO QUICK to tell you when you've done something wrong, but the pair of you are always the FIRST to tell me when I've done something right and that is very rare. I've learned so much from the both of you and I can't thank you enough for adopting me as your tele son. I hope me and Dan are as happy as the pair of you in years to come – maybe with half the rows though. Love you both the world x

To The Sirens – Without you I wouldn't be doing what I do. You're all fucking mental, but I love yas for it. Stop spending your money buying me gifts and buy yourselves a nice top or something. Be good, be safe and be who you wanna be X

To James – What can I say? My best friend for fifteen years. You know me better than I know myself. Thank you for being my best friend. We had the best time and I'll never have times like it again. We were naughty fuckers but we loved it. I'm gutted about what's happened between us and don't even like thinking about it. I can't believe you wasn't there on my wedding day, but it had to be that way. I hope one day we can be friends; we're not there yet, but maybe one day we will be. Good luck with everything you do and I mean that from the bottom of my heart. Be good and find someone who will be good to you. You deserve it x

Photographic Acknowledgments

In order of appearance:

First Plate Section
Page 8 – '*The EsseX Factor* judges' – © EsseX Factor/Bad Influence
    Productions

Second Plate Section
Page 1 – 'From *Signed by Katie* – We could be sisters! – © Andy Neal
Page 3 – 'Where it all began – GO ON THE BLONDE!' –
    © Freemantle Media
Page 5 – 'They day my life changed forever' – © Freemantle Media
Page 6 – 'The Nicole life became quite the thing' – © Freemantle Media
    – '*That* night' – © Greg Brennan
Page 7 – 'Birthday night out with these two . . .' –
    © Dave M Benett/Getty Images
    – 'DYING!' – © Freemantle Media
Page 8 – 'Spice Up Your Life' – © Freemantle Media
    – 'Actually in a bath with Claire from Steps . . .' –
    © Rex/Shutterstock
    – '*CBB* late night fun' – © Rex/Shutterstock
    – 'CHAMP!' – © Stuart Wilson/Getty Images

Third Plate Section
Page 3 – 'The tele mum and dad!' – © Ken McKay/Rex/Shutterstock
Page 4 – 'One of my *Big Brother* press shots' – © Channel 5
    – 'Me and gorgeous Emma' – © Channel 5

All other photographs are author's own.

Every reasonable effort has been made to contact all copyright holders, but if there are any errors or omissions, we will insert the appropriate acknowledgement in subsequent printings of this book.